Ethical Standards for Chemical Dependency Counselors

Ethical Standards for Chemical Dependency Counselors

Second Edition

What They Say
What They Mean
What You Need to Do
Plus 39 Ethical Dilemmas for You to Solve

Nan Franks Richardson and Tim McEnroe

ISBN 1-55691-239-0

Learning Publications, Inc.
5351 Gulf Drive
P.O. Box 1338
Holmes Beach, FL 34218-1338

Printing: 5 4 3 2 1   Year: 06 05 04 03 02

Printed in the United States of America.

Contents

Preface

There's a lot at stake for both professionals and their clients in the development for the professionals of an ethical system that is congruent with their responsibilities as a counselor. Inappropriate ethical choices can lead to a counselor being forbidden to work in the field. And the impact of a counselor's ethical choices can have a profound effect—positive or negative—on the lives of his or her clients. Recognizing this, the accreditation boards of most states require those who seek certification or licensing as chemical dependency professionals to complete a formal course in professional ethics.

This workbook is designed to help those who teach this subject to those who wish to become chemical dependency counselors by supplying a comprehensive study guide and manual that presents and discusses the current ethical standards of our profession. Since the book contains all of the ethical Principles pertaining to credentialed chemical dependency counselors at this time, it will also serve as a handy reminder of the ethical standards for practitioners once they have received their certification.

The book addresses the specific requirements of the revised *Ethical Standards of Credentialed Alcoholism and Drug Abuse Counselors* (adopted in May 1995) and is organized as a discussion of each of its 12 principles. NAADAC's code was chosen for this purpose because it is a national organization and its code is the basis for a number of state codes. The wording in some state codes may be somewhat different, but the intent of all such codes is the same and it is the intent of the codes to which the workbook is addressed. NAADAC has allowed us to reprint each Principle in its entirety; however, NAADAC has not reviewed, participated in the preparation of, or endorsed the materials in it, or the views and conclusions of the authors.

Each chapter concludes with some ethical dilemmas to be thought about by the reader, along with the authors' views about how these dilemmas might be resolved. The book also includes a chapter on ethics for supervisors and a guide counselors may use to analyze ethical dilemmas in a systematic way.

About the Authors

Nan Franks Richardson holds a bachelor's degree in philosophy and a master's degree in rehabilitation counseling. Her credentials include certification as a chemical dependency counselor and as a licensed professional counselor. Especially well-known for her training skills, she conducts workshops on ethics for chemical dependency counselors, post-traumatic stress disorders, and other subjects related to dependency and codependency. She is chief executive officer of the Alcoholism Council of the Cincinnati Area, NCADD.

Tim McEnroe is a writer and consultant. A recovering alcoholic with more than 25 years of sobriety, he has long been active in advocacy efforts aimed at improving treatment and other recovery program opportunities for alcoholics and drug abusers. He has served as president of the Alcoholism Council of the Cincinnati Area, NCADD and received its Weir Goodwin Award for community service in the field of alcoholism.

1
Introduction

What Ethics Are—and What They Are Not

Those who accept the title, privileges, and responsibilities of a certified chemical dependency counselor also agree—whether they know it or not—to adhere to the ethical principles of their profession and to accept oversight and regulation by a national and/or state board.

Each of us reads the *Ethical Standards* and willingly signs allegiance to them with the conviction that we are certainly ethical individuals and will never get into trouble over them or struggle with ethical concerns. Rarely is that the case. What seems simple can actually be quite complex.

Part of the reason for this complexity is the confusion and sometimes conflict between the requirements of our professional ethical standards on the one hand and our personal ethical values and religious convictions and even the law on the other. For some of us the differences are enormous and this means the choices to be made are sometimes extremely difficult.

There are two critical points to keep in mind here:

1. There is a difference—in some cases a substantial difference—between personal values, morals and religious convictions, and our professional ethical standards.

2. Ethical dilemmas that arise in the course of our work as chemical dependency counselors must be resolved by following the guidelines of our professional ethical standards rather than our own personal or religious standards or convictions.

The concept of ethics has been examined since men and women began to think. Unlike religious codes, which are usually said to be handed down from an authority greater than ourselves and are generally thought to be an infallible guide to all human behavior, ethical codes assume a universal philosophical framework concerning human nature and their relationships with one another. The ethicist then examines the possible range of human behavior within that framework, predicts the impact of each choice, and proposes what the best guiding principle ought to be.

Although the thought and discussion that precedes development of these general principles is often hot and heavy, the result is usually a simple one. Aristotle, for instance, stated that ethical behavior should be guided by what he called "the Golden Mean," which states that the ethical action lies between the two possible extremes. According to Aristotle, courage lies between cowardice and rashness, as an example. Kant, on the other hand, summed up ethical behavior through the "categorical imperative," that states that we should act in such a way that if all others would behave in the same way for all time, we would be pleased and the outcome would be positive— essentially the precept of the Christian Golden Rule—"Do unto others as you would have others do unto you."

However simple and logical this may seem, the daily adherence to any ethical principle sometimes generates ethical dilemmas and occasional conflict among us; two thoughtful and well-meaning people can operate from the same principles and yet behave quite differently in a particular situation. A current example is our national debate about extended medical care for the dying. People who share a belief in the sanctity of human life can disagree ardently about sustaining that life through high-tech medical interventions.

Because of such conflicts, those in the profession of drug-abuse counseling—like those in other helping professions—have developed a guiding principle for our professional behavior (the client's interests usually come first) and spelled out 12 specific principles that refer to specific activities.

Ethics and Morals

It is important to remember when thinking about this subject that ethics are not the same as personal values. Our values help us prioritize our life decisions and may vary among us with our personal situations. Frequently, in fact, our values change as our personal situations change. While our values are probably not spelled out explicitly, we and others can tell what they are by observing what we do and say under various circumstances. Most important for this discussion, our personal values may put us in conflict with our professional code or our clients' needs. When they do, substantial ethical problems could arise should we go outside our professional responsibilities and attempt to impose our personal values on our clients as a guide to their behavior. This may, in fact, be the source of the most common of all ethical problems in our field.

Additionally, many of us hold strongly to sets of morals determined by our religious or other convictions that establish "right" and "wrong" behavior. For those who hold them, religious and other moral codes are generally thought to take precedence over current secular thought because of their "higher" source. But moral codes are also not the same thing as professional ethical standards. Adherence to professional ethical standards that seem to violate our religious beliefs or other sources of moral codes can be difficult, even when we know that the standards are generated by esteemed colleagues who are assumed to be upright, objective, knowledgeable, and certainly credible.

Ethics and the Law

Then there is the law. Legal guidelines for professional behavior are developed to protect the professional, the client, and society. Still, what is ethical may not always be what is required by law and in some cases the law may require behavior that seems to be incongruent with our ethical standards. Sometimes the law has not caught up to what is state-of-the-art knowledge in a particular field. In other cases, it may reflect the sometimes uninformed opinions of the community. For the most part, though, current legal requirements and thinking reflect a change on the part of society as a whole with respect to the rights of the individual when they are in conflict with the rights of society or the community. As the country gets more populous and culturally diverse, and as addiction to alcohol and other drugs becomes more pervasive, society is increasingly reaching out to protect itself by shifting priorities from individual rights to community rights. This is reflected in the law and increasingly in ethical codes of the helping professions, including the code for chemical dependency counselors.

Generally focused on confidentiality, client rights, and criminal behavior, problems with the law can arise in our day-to-day professional practice. What do we do when the law is in conflict with our ethical standards? For instance, a client we have finally built trust with tells us that he intends to shoot the neighbor who has been sleeping with his wife. Or, in the course of a counseling session, a client discloses child abuse. Or, a colleague is working with a previous client of ours who we believe to be a habitual liar. These are the kinds of the questions that can keep us up nights as we struggle with the right decision, but this kind of doubt is unnecessary, since each of these dilemmas is covered in the *Ethical Standards* of our profession.

When a conflict arises, responsibility for resolution lies with us as counselors. This book provides a framework for resolution. But remember that difficult ethical choices need not—and most often should not—be made alone. Consultation with supervisors and respected peers should be the rule when in doubt.

Where Our Ethics Come From

Our *philosophy* is the system of beliefs we use that determines how we see our world and the way in which we fit into it. This system governs the way in which we *think.*

Our *ethics* is the system of values we use that determines what behavior is appropriate to our philosophy. This system governs the way we *act.*

Some people believe the world is facing an ethical crisis and that the reason is a lack of ethical judgment. It's not hard to figure out why; just read a newspaper or watch the news on television.

People all over the world are acting in ways that seem fundamentally wrong. A large and respected corporation is found to be selling adulterated baby food. Top executives of a well-respected company are found to have mislead investors and their employees while they reaped huge profits. Lawyers are found to be cheating their clients. A French bureaucrat knowingly lets hundreds of children receive transfusions of AIDS-infected blood. Members of one ethnic group are killing members of another ethnic group in the name of "ethnic cleansing." Parents sell their children for money to buy drugs. The list is endless.

But bad—and real—as these examples are, they are not examples of people who lack ethical systems. Everyone has an ethical system, even those whose activities seem to us to be ethically indefensible. "There is one thing that is terrible," said the film maker Jean Renoir, "and that is that everyone has his reasons."

In the cases noted above, the reasons are, at their core, the result of philosophies most people would see as flawed. A view of the world and your place in it that is essentially antisocial will lead to ethical judgments that result in antisocial behavior.

If you *think* your world is a threateningly hostile place in which everyone is out to get you, your ethical system may permit you to *act* in any way that is likely to help you survive in it.

If you *think* your future well-being depends almost entirely on your making your company profitable, your ethical system may permit you to *act* in any way that is likely to have this effect.

The way we think—our own personal philosophy—is powerfully shaped by our personal experiences and situations; we are all prisoners of our own experiences and hostages to our own perceptions of our own realities. This means the ethical dilemmas each of us has are likely to be the result of whatever perceived dysfunctions in our own lives mold our personal philosophies. If we think we are poorly paid in relation to our training, experience, and responsibilities, our ethical problems are likely to revolve around money. If we think we have unfulfilling sex lives, our ethical problems are likely to revolve around sex.

So, whether you see it that way or not, you have a philosophical system built of your own beliefs and experiences that governs your way of thinking. This way of thinking, in turn, governs the way you act. And since this way of thinking carries over into your work as a chemical-dependency professional, it governs the way you act in relation to your clients, your associates, and your employer.

Who's to Benefit—the Ethical Hierarchy

One of the reasons ethical questions frequently seem difficult is the fact that they require choices, often choices between two or more conflicting interests. In fact, many ethical dilemmas can be solved relatively simply by answering this key question: Whose interests should be put first? That is, in those ethical questions in which interests are in conflict, who should benefit from our decisions?

The basic avowed philosophy of the drug-abuse counseling profession is that the client's interest should be put first. But this is not an unqualified principle. One important qualification is that it is the long-range and not the short-range interests of the client that have primacy. Additionally, the *Ethical Standards* (Principle 7: Client Welfare) acknowledges the fact that society also has a stake in decisions that are made about our clients, and that when matters of "public health, safety, and welfare" are involved, the interests of the public are at least as important as the interests of the client if there is a conflict between them.

This means that there is, in fact, a hierarchy of beneficiaries of our ethical judgments that needs to be considered when conflicts appear. The following is a guide.

1. ***The counselor as a counselor.*** The counselor is an important resource both for society and for a number of individual clients because of his or her training, expertise, special insights, and board certification. For this reason, counselors must refrain from making ethical choices that might deprive society or their other clients of their ability to keep working in the field, even when such choices seem to be in the best interests of an individual client. So when the counselor is faced with an ethical choice that might jeopardize his or her ability to continue to serve as a certified counselor, the choice should be of a course of action that will not allow this to happen. This does not mean we may lie, cheat, or steal in order to preserve our certification. That in itself would be unethical. It simply means that we should not jeopardize our ability to continue to work in our field when making a choice among ethical alternatives.

2. ***Society.*** By requiring certification for people who work as alcohol and other chemical dependency counselors and, in many cases, paying for treatment from public funds, the state in which you work is saying that what you do is important to society as a whole. In turn, by accepting certification from the state in which you work, you become, in effect, a surrogate for society in this important area with responsibility to society for your activities. For this reason, should ethical conflicts arise in which society is one of the potential beneficiaries, the question should be resolved in favor of society. If, for example, you find out during the treatment of a client that he is very likely a mass murderer, you must report your belief to the proper authorities despite rules about confidentiality or the principle of putting clients' welfare first. It is society's right to know this and this right is more important than the client's right to confidentiality.

3. ***The individual client.*** While it may seem strange in a healing profession to put the client's interests third when interests are in conflict, no client's individual interests are sufficiently important to override the interests of society as a whole or the interest of society in assuring that the counselor be able to continue to provide service.

It should be noted that the authors believe that the ethical requirement that counselors protect their ability to serve clients extends beyond what might be considered normal ethical behavior. For example, our profession is characterized by a high degree of burnout of overburdened counselors who have difficulty in distancing themselves from their jobs and client responsibilities We believe that counselor burnout is unethical and should be guarded against by counselors and their employers by assuring plenty of time off, supervisory support, stress seminars, etc.

2
Ethical Principles for Drug-Abuse Professionals

Principle 1: Nondiscrimination

The NAADAC member shall not discriminate against clients or professionals based on race, religion, age, gender, disability, national ancestry, sexual orientation, or economic condition.

a. The NAADAC member shall avoid bringing personal or professional issues into the counseling relationship. Through an awareness of the impact of stereotyping and discrimination, the member guards the individual rights and personal dignity of clients.

b. The NAADAC member shall be knowledgeable about disabling conditions, demonstrate empathy and personal emotional comfort in interactions with clients with disabilities, and make available physical, sensory, and cognition accommodations that allow clients with disabilities to receive services.

Discussion

The *underlying philosophy* of Principle 1 is that professional treatment should be available to everyone who needs and seeks it for the abuse of alcohol and other drugs and that it should not be withheld for any of the reasons spelled out in the principle. It also says we must not withhold cooperation from other professionals for these same reasons.

The *ethical behavior* required by this philosophy is that we as counselors should not withhold our professional services from anyone for these reasons, nor should we withhold our cooperation from anyone we work with for the same reasons.

With most treatment today taking place in public or publicly-supported agencies, the need to learn to feel comfortable with clients with diverse backgrounds is especially important, and perhaps self-evident. Drug abuse is an equal-opportunity disease and thus those who treat it need to be absolutely sure that they provide equal-opportunity treatment.

While most of us believe ourselves to be free of prejudice of any kind, this is rarely the case. Some of us consciously and most of us unconsciously have personal biases of one kind or another against certain individuals who seem unlike ourselves. Often these are remnants of childhood or experiences from which we have inappropriately generalized. Sometimes, too, we recoil from individuals whose problems seem too much like our own, projecting our own unresolved issues on our clients. When we do not want to face the issues in ourselves, we also do not want to face them in a client. All this can lead to discrimination of a very subtle sort.

The need here is to know ourselves well enough to recognize these barriers to our ability to provide appropriate treatment. Once recognized, they can at least be mitigated, perhaps through counseling to ourselves.

Disabilities

The code singles out disability-based discrimination for special attention. Public agencies in particular are seeing an increasing number of people with severe disabilities who seek drug-abuse treatment. In their loneliness and feeling of exclusion from society, those who are physically and mentally disabled are at least as likely as others in our communities to seek solace from legal and illegal drugs.

Principle 3: Competence, covers special skills needed to counsel such people. Principle 1 suggests that even without special skills, we must bring a positive and helping attitude to our relationships with disabled clients, just as we must do in respect to other clients who have other characteristics unlike our own.

Treatment agency managers as well as private practitioners should note the requirement that facilities must be available to accommodate the needs of disabled clients. Federal, state, and local laws and codes require physical access, but providing facilities that accommodate sensory and cognition disabilities needs to be thought through in the context of current and forecasted client profiles.

While individual counselors working for an agency cannot be held personally responsible for violation of the part of the code that requires physical access, they must recognize the code's requirement in this respect and advocate within their agencies for compliance.

All of this seems straightforward enough and for the most part it is. Non-discrimination—especially in providing a needed service—is an important ethical principle for most of us. But as a practical matter in the chemical-dependency field, it is not quite that simple. A number of hypothetical ethical dilemmas are posed below.

Economic Discrimination

It is a fact that lots of men and women in need of and seeking treatment for chemical dependency are denied it every day for economic reasons that are inherently discriminatory according to the code's ethical standards. They have little or no money or insurance to pay for treatment and public treatment facilities are increasingly limited. Thus, treatment is denied in direct violation of this principle.

Those who work for agencies and treatment centers, even though they themselves do not set fees, must work within their organizations for means-based fee schedules.

From the point of view of the individual chemical-dependency professional, however, this is an ethical problem that can be solved only by society as a whole. The nondiscrimination principle applies only to the actions of the individual professional.

On the other hand, Principle 12 requires all counselors to work "to make possible opportunities and choice of service for all human beings of any ethnic or social background whose lives are impaired by alcoholism and drug abuse." Thus while we are not required by this principle to provide these services ourselves, it is an important part of our responsibilities to help society understand the need to provide treatment services to all who can benefit from them.

Ethical Dilemmas

(After you have thought through your own answers to these questions, see the authors' suggested approach to them in Chapter 6.)

1. I have a long and deep-seated aversion to homosexuals. My agency has assigned a chemically dependent man to me for treatment who has told me he is gay. I do not believe I can develop a therapeutic relationship with this man because of my personal aversion. Must I continue to counsel him under these circumstances?

2. My agency has established certain minimum payments required of all clients regardless of their economic circumstances. A long-time client with whom I have been making good progress has just been fired from her job and can no longer pay for treatment. What are my ethical responsibilities to her? To my agency? To me?

3. My administrator has told me to discharge an indigent patient of mine who needs five more days of treatment to make room for an insured patient. I think that is unethical. What should I do?

Principle 1: Nondiscrimination

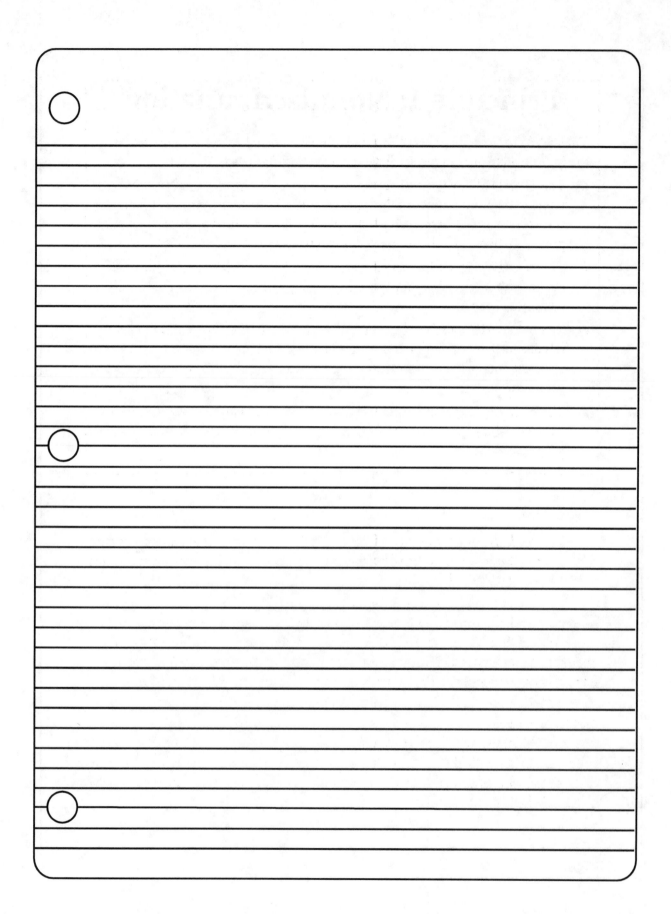

Principle 2: Responsibility

The NAADAC member shall espouse objectivity and integrity, and maintain the highest standards in the services the member offers.

a. The NAADAC member shall maintain respect for institutional policies and management functions of the agencies and institutions within which the services are being performed, but will take initiative toward improving such policies when it will better serve the interest of the client.

b. The NAADAC member, as educator, has a primary obligation to help others acquire knowledge and skills in dealing with the disease of alcoholism and drug abuse.

c. The NAADAC member who supervises others accepts the obligation to facilitate further professional development of those individuals by providing accurate and current information, timely evaluations, and constructive consultation.

d. The NAADAC member who is aware of unethical conduct or of unprofessional modes of practice shall report such inappropriate behavior to the appropriate authority.

Discussion

The *underlying philosophy* of Principle 2 is that the chemical-dependency professional holds a public trust because of her or his training, certification, and commitment to the field.

The *ethical behavior* it requires is personal conduct that serves as a positive example to others, especially in terms of objectivity and personal integrity. In turn, this requires that we use our knowledge and experience to educate others about chemical dependency, and that we must go about the business of helping others in a professional manner consistent with the highest standards in our field.

But the code goes one big step beyond these personal ethical duties of the individual counselor. It also requires that counselors work to assure that the agencies and institutions by which they are employed have and enforce policies and practices consistent with the highest standards of the profession, and that individual counselors take responsibility for reporting activities by other counselors who seem to be acting inappropriately.

This can be a heavy burden, and the reason is contained in the word "espouse" in the first paragraph of the principle.

"Espouse" means "take up, support, or advocate." It means, in other words, both talking the talk and walking the walk.

One problem here is that it is difficult—and perhaps impossible—for chemical dependency professionals to separate their personal and professional lives. As a perhaps obvious example, this principle at least implies that a chemical dependency counselor—recovering or not—has an ethical obligation to refrain from the abuse of drugs—including alcohol—even in private and when not acting in a professional capacity. If we do not behave in our personal lives in a way that is congruent with what we teach in our professional lives, our ability to help our clients reshape their own lives is diminished because of inconsistencies in our own.

Thus, the counselor should strive to live a sober life in the fullest meaning of the term: being honest and fair in all dealings with others, being objective and nonjudgmental in his or her personal and professional relationships, and honestly and forthrightly facing up to personal problems. Accepting responsibility for our behavior as an example to others, and helping clients accept responsibility for theirs, is one of the ethical points of Principle 2.

Organizational Responsibilities

Beyond this, we have the obligation to insist that the organizations we work for and the individuals we work with maintain this same high standard of responsibility. This means two things:

1. Advocacy within our organizations when we see inappropriate policies or activities. This is rarely easy. The appropriate way to go about this is to do so through existing management channels. It is important to note here that the code recognizes the limitations of the authority of the individual counselor in this respect. That is, we are responsible for trying to get appropriate changes made, but unless we have the authority to actually make the change, our responsibility does not go beyond that. On the other hand, should the inappropriate policy require the individual counselor to act unethically or otherwise inappropriately, it may be necessary to resign if it is not changed.

2. Reporting those individuals whose activities are detrimental to their clients and the profession to the appropriate authorities can be an equally unpleasant responsibility. And unlike the responsibility to work within our own organizations for change, we are ourselves responsible for carrying it out. This is not an activity most people look upon with much enthusiasm, but it is necessary because coun-

selors acting inappropriately can do grave harm to their clients. They can also do grave harm to the agencies for which they work, since the agencies are responsible for the professional activities of those they employ. Because of the seriousness of some forms of unethical or otherwise inappropriate behavior and its possible impact on both the clients and the employer, individual counselors should stay within institutional-management channels in these cases, at least unless it becomes clear that the institution is not going to act on its own. But the responsibility for taking the first step remains with the individual counselor.

Ethical standards for supervisors are discussed in a separate chapter.

Ethical Dilemmas

(After you have thought through your own answers to these questions, see the authors' suggested approach to them in Chapter 6.)

4. I am married and having an affair with a man I love very much. He is not a client and is not connected in any way with my agency. My husband travels a great deal and my lover and I are careful to avoid meeting when he is in town or where we might be seen by people who know us. I do not want to leave my husband, but this other relationship gives me more confidence and personal fulfillment than I have ever had before. I do not see how it is hurting anyone or how it affects me professionally. Is it ethically proper for me to continue this affair?

5. My agency has not been able to give anyone a raise in two years and I've got a family to support. I have been offered a part-time job running a program for another agency. This would supplement my income with money I really need. I can do both jobs if I use my weekends, sick days, and comp time from my agency to run the program for the other agency. Is it ethically okay for me to take this second job?

6. I am a chemical dependency counselor in a drug-treatment facility that is part of a hospital. A long-time alcoholic has come to us for treatment. I believe we can help him into recovery, but only as an inpatient. The problem is that his company's insurance does not cover enough inpatient treatment for alcoholism to do him much good, but he does have coverage for inpatient psychiatric treatment. The people who run the psychiatric unit say they will admit him if we can get this past his insurance company. We can do this by wording our diagnosis to make it appear that he has a number of treatable psychiatric symptoms, though the fact is he does not. If we do this, he will get treatment. If we don't, he probably won't. What is required under this principle?

7. I never use or abuse substances when I'm working or even when I'm about to go to work, but my live-in partner and I do sometimes smoke marijuana and get pretty high on alcohol from time to time. This is always when we're alone or with friends at parties. I'm not a recovering person and my clients never see me using, let alone impaired. Why shouldn't I be able to do these things that millions of others do simply because of my job?

Principle 2: Responsibility

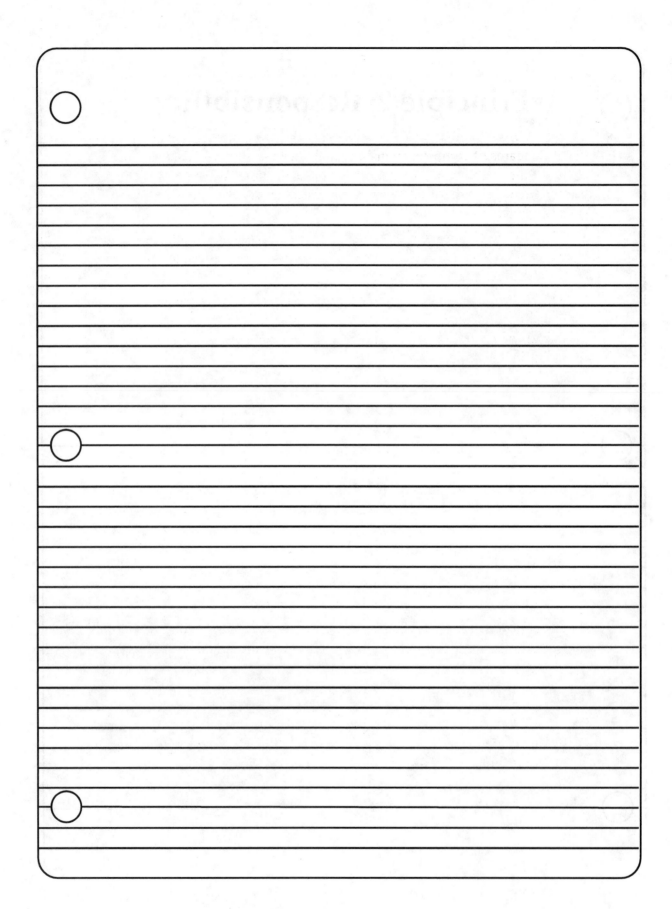

Principle 3: Competence

The NAADAC member shall recognize that the profession is founded on national standards of competency that promote the best interests of society, of the client, of the member, and of the profession as a whole. The NAADAC member shall recognize the need for ongoing education as a component of professional competency.

a. The NAADAC member shall recognize boundaries and limitations of the member's competencies and not offer services or use techniques outside of these professional competencies.

b. The NAADAC member shall recognize the effect of impairment on professional performance and shall be willing to seek appropriate treatment for oneself or for a colleague. The member shall support peer-assistance programs in this respect.

Discussion

The *underlying philosophy* of this principle is that we should be willing to accept that there is a national set of treatment-competency standards that support the best interests of all affected by chemical dependency counseling—the client, professional, and society as a whole. Embodied in this acceptance is the willingness to hold ourselves and others to these standards, but to understand and accept the limitations of what we actually know how to do. It also demands of us that we recognize that the field of chemical dependency and the larger field of behavioral health are dynamic, and that we ourselves are ever-changing, fallible human beings, requiring continuing self-examination and education.

The *ethical behavior* it requires is an active role in our own adherence to this principle. The specific requirement is to understand the limitations of our own competence and not overstep those limitations in our counseling. This is not always easy to do. Individuals who come to us for counseling often have problems, disorders, or impairments besides chemical dependency. It is a very human tendency to want to deal with issues as they come up. Sometimes we can do so competently and sometimes we do not really have the training or experience to do so in a professional manner. When we do not, we must not try.

Dual Diagnosis

In many cases we see clients who have a "dual diagnosis" or "co-occurring disorder." A "dual diagnosis" occurs when an individual is affected by both a drug-abuse disorder or chemical dependency and an emotional or psychiatric illness. Both disorders may affect the individual physically, psychologically, socially, and spiritually and present symptoms that interfere with life functioning and interact with one another, making each symptom more severe.

Many chemical dependency counselors do not have the training to deal with the emotional or psychiatric disorder involved. Too often, the additional diagnosis or problem is not discovered at intake or even early in treatment. In other cases it is revealed only after a lengthy period of recovery, seemingly emerging when we least expect it. Many addicts have sincerely tried to recover from chemical dependency only to be overwhelmed by their emotional illnesses and relapse.

Chemical dependency counselors need to develop the ability to identify co-occurring disorders and the maturity and discipline to ask for help from those who are trained to treat such illnesses. In some cases this calls for a referral to another counselor, perhaps one in another specialty. In other cases, it may be that the client's disorders are so complex that treatment by another agency is called for.

This is often not an easy call to make. Many—perhaps most—substance abusers are clinically depressed as well as being addicted to the chemical they are abusing. Withdrawal from the chemical in some cases worsens the depression. Counselors need to be especially sensitive to this possibility and make sure they have the kind of supervision available to them that will guide them in making good decisions about treatment.

Additionally, studies show that a large percentage of those with more complex mental illnesses are also chemical abusers, often preferring the effects of alcohol and illegal drugs to the side effects of the psychotropic drugs that have been prescribed for them. It is very important that such clients be treated by those who are trained to do so.

Couples Counseling

A seemingly more benign area in which a possible lack of competence could lead to inappropriate treatment is couples counseling.

Many drug abusers who come to us for counseling have troubled relationships with their life partners. There are probably few, indeed, who do not. In many cases we as chemical dependency counselors can help them find a way to make such relationships more healthy. Recovery itself could very well be the answer. But it could also be the case that the relationship problems are well beyond our training to address. In such cases, referral to a specialist in couples counseling is the ethically responsible thing to do.

Cultural Competence

Another form of competence not addressed specifically in the code but important nonetheless is cultural competence. This is especially important for counselors in public agencies.

The symptoms and resulting problems of drug abuse are similar regardless of the culture of the person experiencing them, but diagnosis and appropriate treatment may not be. While this is undergoing some change, the fact is that most counselors in most agencies are from the majority culture, yet in many cases in public agencies at least, the clients are not. An increasing number of agencies are requiring training to lead to an understanding of cultural differences that could impact treatment methods. This recognizes that effective treatment requires something beyond empathy and nondiscrimination. It often requires specific knowledge of attitudes and treatment methods that are culturally specific.

These differences are often seen as racial, but this is not always the case. Substance-abusing gay men and lesbians, for example, often experience difficulty in getting effective treatment when counselors do not understand the culture in which they live their lives.

Besides training, in order to practice within our own limits we must have the personal maturity to judge ourselves accurately, seeking feedback through appropriate colleagues or supervisors in order to assess our strengths, weaknesses, knowledge, and skill. Since insight without action is rarely beneficial, we must be willing to seek help when it is needed.

Peer Assistance

Many of us assume that because we have achieved abstinence from alcohol and/or other drugs we are beyond impairment, ignoring other difficulties such as codependency, compulsive disorders, anxiety, and depression. Although we counsel others to intervene with friends and family members, we hesitate when faced with the addiction of a coworker or boss. Although we advocate for compassion and treatment for those we class as clients, we too often feel anger, disgust, or smugness when faced with chemical addiction, codependency, or emotional problems in our colleagues.

The rate of relapse among recovering chemical dependency counselors is high. Many of us know counselors who, after years of sobriety, relapsed and died or continue to struggle, unable to find their way back to recovery. It is critical that we continue to support one another in the need for attention to our own health.

Ethical Dilemmas

(After you have thought through your own answers to these questions, see the authors' suggested approach to them in Chapter 6.)

8. I have a client who presents his major relapse trigger as arguments he has with his wife about the way their money is used. He has asked me to see them together and act as a mediator so that he can get his feelings expressed in a more neutral place. From what he says, I can see that this dispute would create lots of tension and I think that I could help. Should I see them?

9. One of the counselors I work with claims to be recovering and talks a lot about AA, but a couple of times in the last couple of weeks I've seen him coming out of a bar in what looks clearly to me to be an intoxicated state. He's a good friend of mine. Does this principle mean I have to report him?

10. I was recently asked to make a presentation to a group one of my co-counselors runs. As I was waiting to make my presentation I had a chance to watch him work with the group for the first time. It was apparent to me very quickly that he was over his head and potentially injuring his clients by opening emotional wounds without allowing any way for them to be closed. I really doubt that he's competent to run this or any other group. What do I do about it?

11. Part of my caseload is an Hispanic-American drug abuser. His English is good and we have little or no trouble understanding the words we use when we speak to each other. But we both get frustrated sometimes because he feels that the suggestions I make to him about changes in his life are things that might make him an outsider in the world in which he lives most of his life. What should I do?

Principle 3: Competence

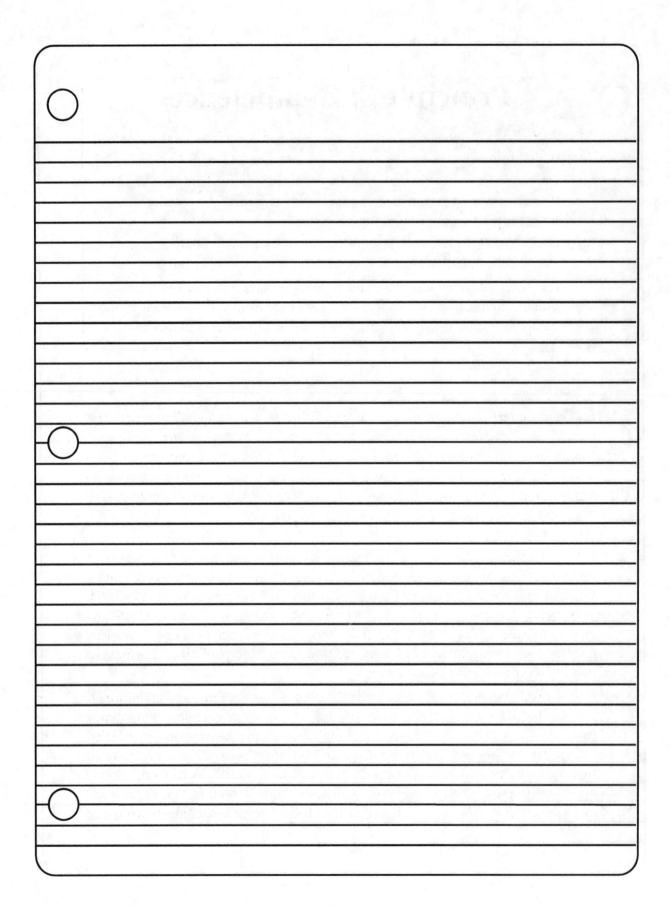

Principle 4: Legal and Moral Standards

The NAADAC member shall uphold the legal and accepted moral codes that pertain to professional conduct.

a. The NAADAC member shall be fully cognizant of all federal laws and laws of the member's respective state government regarding the practice of alcoholism and drug-abuse counseling.

b. The NAADAC member shall not claim, either directly or by implication, professional qualifications/affiliations that the member does not possess.

c. The NAADAC member shall ensure that products and services associated with or provided by the member by means of teaching, demonstration, publications, or other types of media meet the ethical standards of this code.

Discussion

The *underlying philosophy* of Principle 4 is that the credentialing process invests those who are awarded certification with a form of professional legitimacy. Counselors must live by the codes and laws that govern the profession. Should they use this legitimacy to claim or imply more than it actually means, or to seem to give products or services the appearance of legitimacy they don't deserve, they can harm both the people who accept these claims and the profession by threatening its credibility.

The *ethical behavior* required by this philosophy is absolute truthfulness in representations the individual counselor makes about her or his professional qualifications and about professional products with which the counselor is associated. This means that counselors should not exaggerate the extent of their credentialing or competence, or use their credentials or professional memberships to mislead people about the usefulness of books, tests, teaching tools, and other treatment or training tools they're associated with.

As we have discussed earlier, it is the clear message of this and other principles in the Standards that the work of alcohol and other chemical dependency counselors is a form of public trust that puts special requirements on credentialed counselors for honesty and truthfulness in both their personal and professional lives beyond that which might be required of those in other lines of work. This is necessary to preserve the credibility of the profession as well as that of the individual counselor, and the well-being of the client. Even a few credentialed counselors claiming more for themselves, their services, or books than they can actually deliver can injure the entire profession.

The requirement of this principle to abide by all legal codes can be especially tricky. This is so because the requirements of the laws regarding what we do can seem in some cases to be in conflict with ethical behavior.

The trickiness of the legal codes and in some cases the conflict between the legal codes and ethical standards is one of many reasons why counselors should never address substantial ethical questions or any legal question without consultation with supervisors or respected peers. We live in a litigious society in which both counselors and their employers can and frequently are held responsible for their actions and decisions, some of which may seem trivial at the time they are made. The prudent counselor will always check with experienced and informed others before taking action on ethical matters.

Additionally, the requirement that conduct uphold "accepted moral codes" at a time when virtually any kind of conduct seems to be accepted can look like a convenient loophole to someone searching for one. Counselors should not be mislead by this, for it is the accepted moral codes "which pertain to professional conduct" that must be upheld under this principle. These are more rigid than those often applied to day-to-day behavior by the society in which we live. "I'm only doing what everyone else is doing" is not acceptable when what everyone is doing is unethical or illegal.

An example of this that should be obvious is the use by counselors of illegal drugs. It may be tempting for a counselor who is not himself a recovering person to think that a relaxing hit on a marijuana cigarette in the privacy of his own home at the end of a stressful day would be a fine and allowable thing. It is not, because the possession of marijuana is illegal and thus prohibited by this ethical standard.

Ethical Dilemmas

(After you have thought through your own answers to these questions, see the authors' suggested approach to them in Chapter 6.)

12. I'm a board-credentialed counselor who has made a specialty of treating battered and abused women. Someone I work with—also a board-credentialed counselor—has been working on a book on this subject, but really doesn't have much experience in this special field. I've given him lots of ideas, but I've never seen the actual book. He now says that his publisher wants the name of an author on it who has lots of experience in the field to give it credibility. He wants me to agree to put my name on it as coauthor with his but says there isn't time for me to read and comment on the book itself. He's willing to share the money with me

and I'm reasonably sure he's done a good job. Can I lend my name to this project?

13. The program I work for has decided to advertise for clients for a new codependency group and wants me to lead it. Although I know the basic dynamics of chemically dependent families and have read a couple of self-help books, I've really had no training in codependency. Is this a misrepresentation of my qualifications? How should I handle the situation?

14. My agency provides services to unemployed recovering people, mostly job counseling. Because I am a credentialed chemical dependency counselor, the agency says in its grant applications that we provide chemical dependency treatment. Since I am the only credentialed person here and treatment at this point is not part of my job, this is not actually the case. This strikes me as unethical. What should I do?

Principle 4: Legal and Moral Standards

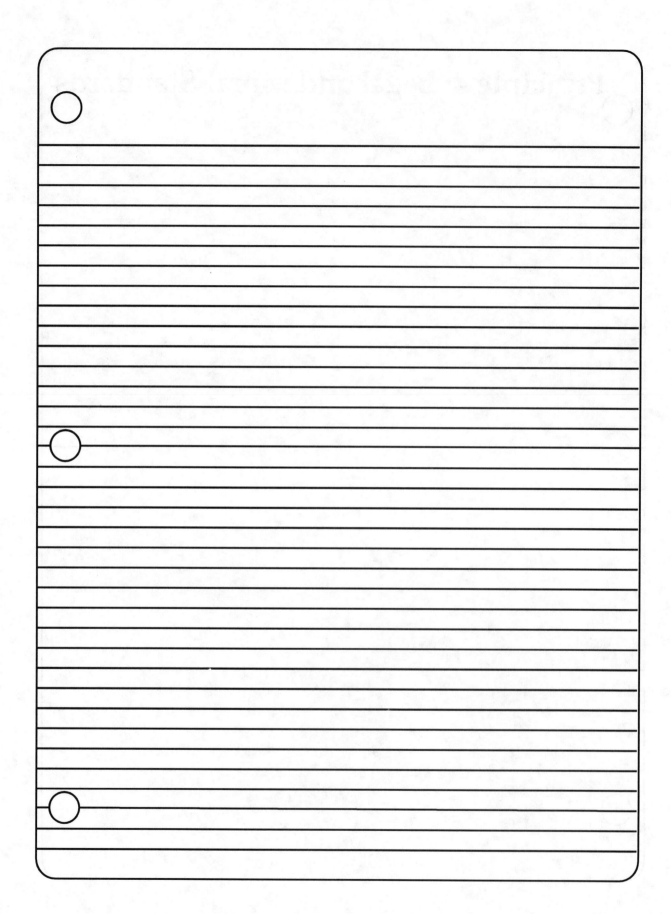

Principle 5: Public Statements

The NAADAC member shall honestly respect the limits of present knowledge in public statements concerning alcoholism and drug abuse.

a. The NAADAC member, in making statements to clients, other professionals, and the general public shall state as fact only those matters that have been empirically validated as fact. All other opinions, speculations, and conjecture concerning the nature of alcoholism and drug abuse, its natural history, its treatment, or any other matters which touch on the subject of alcoholism and drug abuse shall be represented as less than scientifically validated.

b. The NAADAC member shall acknowledge and accurately report the substantiation and support for statements made concerning the nature of alcoholism and drug abuse, its natural history, and its treatment. Such acknowledgment should extend to the source of the information and reliability of the method by which it was derived.

Discussion

The *underlying philosophy* of this principle is that the field of chemical-dependency treatment is dynamic rather than static and that the consumer (community, client, etc.) has a right to accurately reported, documented, and represented material, whether it be information or skill-based training.

The *ethical behavior* required by this principle is that counselors must state facts as facts, opinions as opinions, and feelings as feelings. Personal experience may be entirely valid but must be represented as such. It can be tempting to endorse enthusiastically or to write off opinions other than our own as ridiculous without stating why or citing the research that validates our contradictory views. Pressure from ourselves or our organizations to succeed can tempt us to represent ourselves as having expertise where none exists. It is important to resist all such temptations.

At the same time, complicated as we know it is, the huge number of self-help books on the market today often give the impression that more is known about the disease than actually is, or that there are short-cuts to successful treatment that on professional analysis turn out to be false or unproven.

Part of the chemical dependency counselor's job (see Principle 2: Responsibility) is to help keep the field as free as possible of exaggeration and misrepresen-

31

tation. This obviously refers most specifically to ourselves. When we educate or otherwise give instruction or information, we need to be as sure as we can be that what we are saying has objective validity.

Additionally, since what is known changes and in some cases what was thought to be known is not true, it is crucial that we continually evaluate the limits of our knowledge, skills, and training and accept the need for continuing training and self-education to keep current with contemporary knowledge and experience.

Ethical Dilemmas

(After you have thought through your own answers to these questions, see the authors' suggested approach to them in Chapter 6.)

15. I think it is ridiculous that some people continue to question that alcoholism and drug dependence is a disease. In providing community education, can't I just say that it has definitely been proven that it is a disease?

16. I recently took a six-hour course in basic drug-abuse counseling. At the end of the course the trainer said that I and the rest of the class were now prepared to go out and counsel people ourselves. It seems to me after taking this course that treatment is actually much more complicated than I thought it was and I feel less qualified to give treatment now than I was at the start because I have more questions about it. I think that telling beginners like me that we're prepared to give treatment as a result of this brief class is unethical. Is it? What should I do?

17. I am personally convinced by what I have read and observed that addiction is primarily genetic. When I get family of origin information, I nearly always find drug abuse in prior generations. When I don't I'm sure it's because the person I'm assessing is either lying or uninformed. Why don't we simply assume that this is true from the evidence we have and find ways to deal with it?

Principle 5: Public Statements

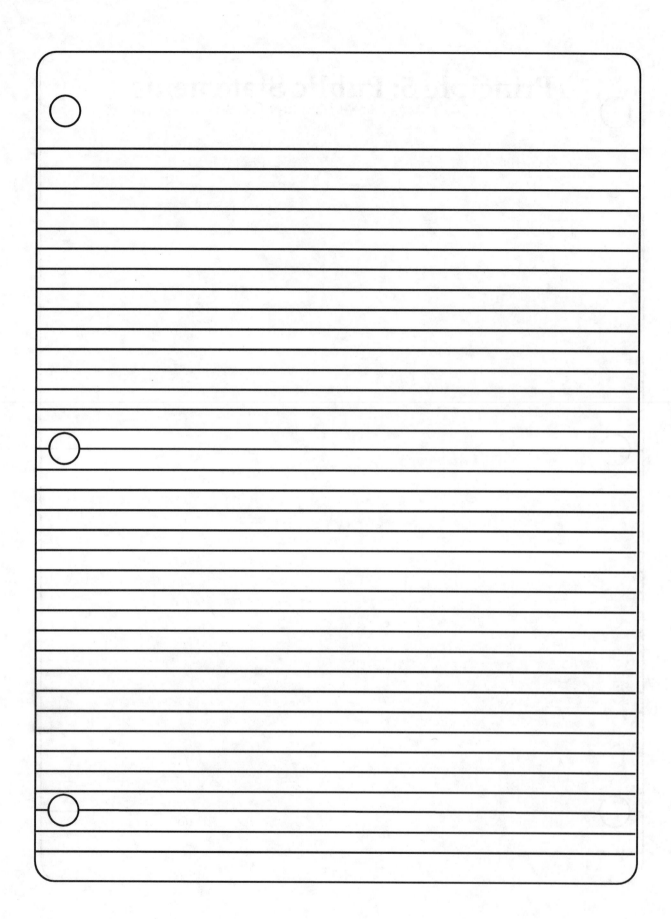

Principle 6: Publication Credit

The NAADAC member shall assign credit to all who have contributed to the published material and for the work upon which the publication is based.

a. The NAADAC member shall recognize joint authorship and major contributions of a professional nature made by one or more persons to a common project. The author who has made the principal contribution to a publication must be identified as first author.

b. The NAADAC member shall acknowledge in footnotes or in an introductory statement minor contributions of a professional nature, extensive clerical or similar assistance, and other minor contributions.

c. The NAADAC member shall in no way violate the copyright of anyone by reproducing material in any form whatsoever, except in those ways that are allowed under the copyright laws. This involves direct violation of copyright as well as the passive assent to the violation of copyright by others.

Discussion

The *underlying philosophy* of this principle is that appropriate credit for material, insights, and work should be given when and to whom it is due, and that counselors should spell out in their own publications the source of all contributions to it either intellectually or with work such as proofreading and typing.

The *ethical behavior* required by the principle is to be scrupulous in giving acknowledgment and recognition to all contributors to any publication on which the counselor works and that the counselor should not claim credit for work done by others or ideas originally conceived by someone else.

This is obviously of greatest importance to counselors who write and teach in the field. Both theory and practice of alcohol and drug-abuse treatment and prevention are in a continual state of evolution and much is being written and taught about them. Some of this work is original and some is derivative. Those to whom information is communicated have a right to know its source, and those who create it have a right to credit for their work.

Additionally, because drug abuse is so widespread and many seek both personal insights and professional training in the field, there is an active market for literature and seminars and other class work, so the temptation to publish and teach is great. This principle holds that counselors who seek to fill these needs do not pass off what is in effect the intellectual property of others as their own.

Ethical Dilemmas

(After you have thought through your own answers to these questions, see the authors' suggested approach to them in Chapter 6.)

18. I teach a course in counseling to candidates for certification. I've been at it for a long time and have accumulated a number of pieces from various sources that I photocopy and hand out to my students to reinforce points that I make during my training. They're mostly portions of articles and parts of books. In some cases they're things I've picked up at seminars I've attended and I don't even know the actual source. Must I give full credit to those whose material I pass around? What if I don't know the source?

19. I've just finished writing a book on treating adolescent drug abusers after working as a counselor in a treatment center for eight years. I've read a lot in the field and kept up with the literature. I believe the basic ideas in my book are mine and I certainly didn't copy anything from anyone. But at this point in my professional life it's not very clear to me what is a new idea to me and what I've learned in one way or another from others. How do I give credit under these circumstances?

Principle 6: Publication Credit

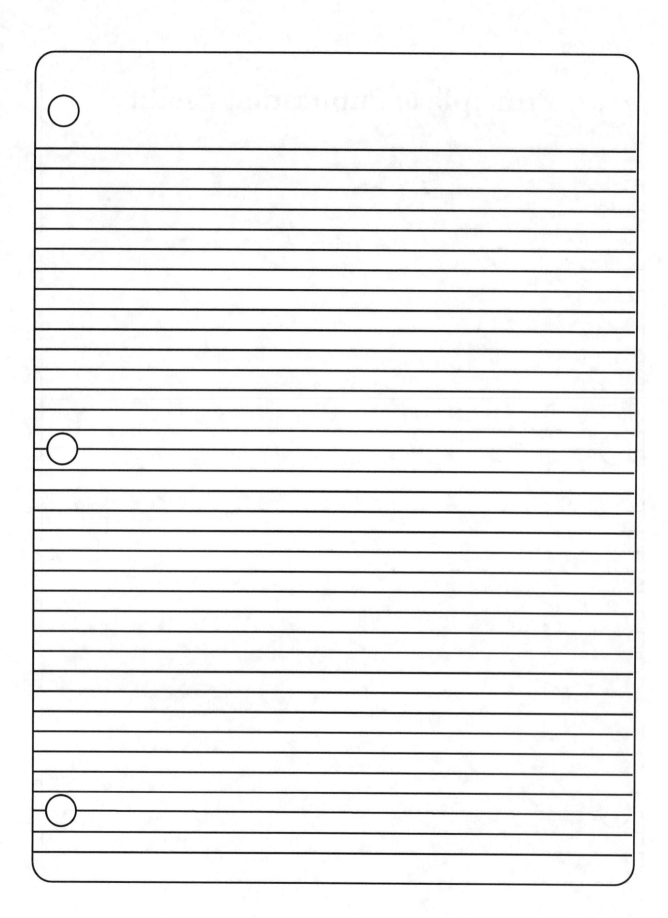

Principle 7: Client Welfare

The NAADAC member shall promote the protection of the public health, safety, and welfare and the best interest of the client as a primary guide in determining the conduct of all NAADAC members.

a. The NAADAC member shall disclose the member's code of ethics, professional loyalties, and responsibilities to all clients.

b. The NAADAC member shall terminate a counseling or consulting relationship when it is reasonably clear to the member that the client is not benefiting from the relationship.

c. The NAADAC member shall hold the welfare of the client paramount when making any decisions or recommendations concerning referral, treatment procedures, or termination of treatment.

d. The NAADAC member shall not use or encourage a client's participation in any demonstration, research, or other nontreatment activities when such participation would have potential harmful consequences for the client or when the client is not fully informed. (See Principle 9.)

e. The NAADAC member shall take care to provide services in an environment that will ensure the privacy and safety of the client at all times and ensure the appropriateness of service delivery.

Discussion

Frightening as it may seem, the *underlying philosophy* of this principle is that we are, within the scope of our professional relationships, personally responsible for protecting the welfare of the clients with whom we work, either as individuals or members of a group.

The *ethical behavior* required of this principle is that we as counselors take upon ourselves responsibility for assuring the safety and overall welfare of the client.

This principle is a good example of the way in which both the law and ethical codes are putting the responsibilities of licensed counselors to "promote the protection of the public health, safety, and welfare" ahead of the best interests of the client in guiding our work. Prior to the current revision, this principle said simply that, "The alcoholism and chemical dependency counselor should respect the integrity and protect the welfare of the person or group with whom the counselor is working," that is, the client or clients in group situations. Putting the public interest first is a dramatic change, and in line with contemporary thinking about the rights of society *vs.* the rights of individuals. This point was discussed in more detail in the section on ethical hierarchy in the introductory chapter.

Both idealistic new counselors and more experienced professionals who began their careers in the period in which client interests alone were given consideration often find this relatively new requirement a difficult one to accept. But the ethical code here, backed up in many cases by the law, is unambiguous and must be followed.

It should be remembered, too, that the client interests that were to be protected under previous codes and customs were long-range rather than short-range. Not reporting a client whom we believe to be about to commit a serious crime may protect him in the short run, but in the long run he is likely to get caught and go to jail, as well as injuring someone else either financially or physically. Thus making the required report is ethically correct, because doing so protects both society and the long-range interests of the client.

The decision to report or not report a crime that a client is likely to commit is another that counselors should not make on their own. Supervisors or respected peers should always be consulted before this step is taken.

Neutral Outcomes Not Enough

Despite the popular mandate "when in doubt, do no harm," a neutral outcome in therapeutic counseling is not enough. As certified chemical dependency counselors, what we do professionally is expected to be helpful and we should work out minimum standards for progress with each client and end any relationship that is not at least meeting this goal.

One of the most frequent violations of ethical codes, in fact, is continuing treatment beyond the point at which it is helpful to clients. There are many reasons for this, but the most frequent is financial.

For private practitioners, the question of why terminate a client who seems to enjoy the relationship and always pays her bills is often a difficult one. Other common reasons for continuing treatment longer than is useful to clients are equally unethical; we enjoy the client's company, find him or her attractive physically or intellectually, etc.

But with treatment shifting more and more to public agencies, financial considerations of the organization are also the most common reason for continuing a client relationship beyond the point of usefulness. Agencies now are generally paid on a "capitation" basis, which means they receive a certain amount of money for each client in treatment. When the client is terminated, the capitation payment goes away. Many agencies are hard-pressed for funds and for this reason want to keep their client loads as heavy as possible. Sometimes this means keeping clients longer than is appropriate.

As is the case in other situations in which the individual counselor believes his or her employer is acting unethically, the counselor has the ethical duty to point this out, always going within management channels. Ultimately, though, it is the employer rather than the counselor who is responsible for correcting the situation.

Client Self-Reliance Is the Goal

Counselors need to remind themselves over and over again that the objective of treatment is the development of rational self-reliance on the part of the client. Reliance on the counselor may be better than reliance on drugs, but cannot be seen as a treatment goal.

On the other hand, too quick termination or referral is also unethical according to this principle. Some clients are inherently more difficult than others. Referring a difficult client to another counselor is sometimes appropriate and sometimes not. Certainly not every counselor/client match is going to produce satisfactory results. But difficult clients are often the ones from whom we learn the most and referrals and terminations of clients because they are difficult need to be done only after careful thought and consultation.

Counselor Safety

There are, however, situations in which either referrals or termination is required. For the most part, these involve counselor safety. More and more clients with dual diagnosis of mental illness and drug abuse are being seen by public agencies. In some cases, mentally-ill clients become physically or emotionally threatening to their counselors. While this is rare, when it does happen the counselor has the ethical right and we believe a duty to insist upon either a referral or termination. The counselor's safety is more important than the client's continued treatment, at least by that agency.

Role Play

No matter how tempting, using a client in a role-play or demonstration situation can be dangerous. To avoid potential damage, we and our clients must be able to judge how the experience will impact the client after the event. It is easy to forget that our clients want to please us and will agree to anything they think might benefit us or our programs. In a field filled with participation in 12-step programs, self-disclosure can seem commonplace and an opportunity to grow. But it is the emotional impact that may follow self-disclosure that can send a fragile recovery into relapse. Even when using other professionals in a training demonstration, careful consideration must be given by all concerned to the potential impact.

This is another area in which consultation with supervisors or respected peers is essential. Hard as we try to be objective and "professional" about ourselves and about our clients, it is often not easy to judge when actions we want to pursue are helpful to our client or merely convenient for ourselves.

Role-play and demonstration situations are fairly obvious examples, but motivations in referral and termination decisions may also need to be examined.

Client welfare is also dependent on the provision of services in a safe and private environment. With many agencies stretched for space and time, it is sometimes too easy to ignore the rights of clients in this respect. These needs are discussed more thoroughly in the next chapter.

Ethical Dilemmas

(After you have thought through your own answers to these questions, see the authors' suggested approach to them in Chapter 6.)

20. I've been working with a client in my private practice for over a year. For the last several months he has kept his appointments, paid his bills on time, and talks a lot, but I don't really feel like he is getting any better or addressing real issues. I've talked to him about the possibility of discontinuing counseling, and he says I'm the only friend he has. Since it's his choice to come, I've continued to see him, but I question whether I should. What should I do ethically?

21. I have been working for several weeks with a client who is new to the agency. She admits that she is a crack addict, but refuses to take any of my suggestions for attending meetings, finding a sponsor, or even taking care of herself physically. I've about had it with her and would like to refer her to someone who might be able to get through to her. May I do so?

22. I am a credentialed chemical dependency counselor and am working on my masters degree. I have chosen as my thesis subject the usefulness of alternative treatment methods and need to do practical research to validate my points. I work in a treatment facility and have plenty of clients I'm sure would volunteer for the experiments. May I use them?

Principle 7: Client Welfare

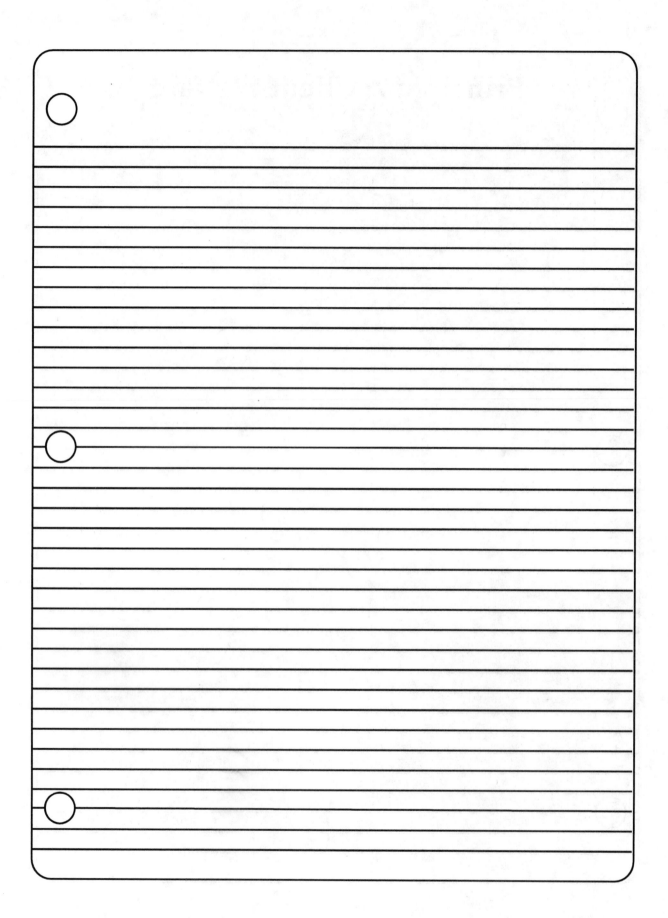

Principle 8: Confidentiality

The NAADAC member working in the best interest of the client shall embrace, as a primary obligation, the duty of protecting clients' rights under confidentially and shall not disclose confidential information acquired in teaching, practice, or investigation without appropriately executed consent.

a. The NAADAC member must provide the client his or her rights regarding confidentiality in writing as part of informing the client of any areas likely to affect the client's confidentially. This includes the recording of the clinical interviews, the use of material for insurance purposes, the use of material for training or observation by another party.

b. The NAADAC member shall make appropriate provisions for the maintenance of confidentially and the ultimate disposition of confidential records. The member shall ensure that data obtained, including any form of electronic communication, are secured by the available security methodology. Data shall be limited to information that is necessary and appropriate to the services being provided and be accessible only to appropriate personnel.

c. The NAADAC member shall adhere to all federal and state laws regarding confidentially and the member's responsibility to report clinical information in specific circumstances to the appropriate authorities.

d. The NAADAC member shall discuss the information obtained in clinical, consulting, or observational relationships only in the appropriate setting for professional purposes that are in the client's best interest. Written and oral reports must present only data germane and pursuant to the purpose of evaluation, diagnosis, progress, and compliance. Every effort shall be made to avoid undue invasion of privacy.

e. The NAADAC member shall use clinical and other material in teaching and/or in writing only when there is no identifying information used about the parties involved.

Discussion

The *underlying philosophy* of this principle is that a therapeutic relationship between counselor and client can take place only in an atmosphere in which the client can be assured that information given to the counselor will be used entirely for the benefit of the client. But it also acknowledges that this right to confidentiality is qualified and does not extend to information gained by the counselor that may indicate potential harm to the client or others.

The *ethical behavior* required by this philosophy is that the counselor must protect information gained in the course of his or her professional life about a client from either purposeful or accidental disclosure to others. But in those cases when what the counselor learns clearly indicates the possibility of danger to the client or others, it requires disclosure to the appropriate authorities or other persons.

Confidentiality is among the most important traditions of any form of counseling. This is the case because the counselor can help only those clients who feel sufficiently safe with the counselor to divulge and discuss the most sensitive aspects of their lives without fear that this information will be used in a way that could harm them. This high degree of safety can be assured only if the counselor makes it clear to each client that confidentiality will be maintained and then adheres to the letter and spirit of this principle.

But there is more at stake in maintaining confidentiality than a client's emotional safety. We live in a violent society and many who seek treatment for drug addiction are targets for violent behavior. The most obvious of these are women in treatment facilities who are victims of abusive relationships and fleeing their abusers. For the physical protection of such clients, it is very important that the location of the facility and who is a resident there be guarded from all those who do not legally need this information.

A Complex Issue

Important as it is, the principle of confidentiality is becoming an increasingly complicated issue for counselors, particularly for chemical dependency counselors.

This is the case for five important reasons:

1. Unlike counselors in other helping profession specialties, the behavior of drug-abuse counselors on this issue is governed by federal law, rather than state law.

2. In general, there is a strong conflict between traditional interpretations of confidentiality, ethical requirements, and the law as it exists today in virtually every state, in which client rights to privacy are secondary to the rights of society to safety.

3. The increasing reliance on electronic transmission of documents presents significant challenges on both ends of the communication trail.

4. The increasing conglomeration of treatment facilities and agencies into fewer and larger units encourages the mingling of client records and enlarges the number of people who have access to them.

5. The increasing use of managed care to hold down treatment costs also enlarges the number of people with access to client records.

Federal Law

As indicated above, federal laws set forth the confidentiality requirements for chemical dependency counselors. These laws apply to all counselors who work for "federally assisted" organizations or with "federally assisted" clients. Since "federally assisted includes Internal Revenue Service nonprofit status for provider organizations and Social Security or Medicare benefits for clients, the reach of "federally assisted" is very broad.

The general federal rule about confidentiality is that a program and counselor may not disclose any information about any patient to anyone, with certain specific exceptions. These exceptions are:

- internal (intra-agency) communications
- information in which clients are not identified
- with proper consent (see below)
- to other qualified agencies with which formal agreements exist
- in medical emergencies
- for research/audit purposes
- as a result of a court order
- in the event of the threat of a crime on program premises or against program personnel
- when reporting suspected child abuse and neglect

The difference between the federal confidentiality law governing substance-abuse counselors and state laws governing other counselors can be troublesome and needs careful consideration.

In most cases, the most restrictive law applies. In December 2000, Congress passed the Privacy Standards for the Health Insurance Portability and Accountability Act (HIPAA). These privacy standards now hold all health-care related organizations to very strict standards regarding privacy and confidentiality of client records.

While the federal confidentiality standards for alcohol and other drug-abuse services apply only to those receiving federal assistance, these new rules apply to all providers of these services, regardless of whether they receive federal assistance or not. Although AOD counselors are already held to strict standards, the new rules require greater scrutiny of oral, electronic, and written communications and the security of client information and contain more penalties for violation.

Duty to Warn

The major point on which federal and state confidentiality laws disagree is on the "duty to warn." Under most state laws and ethical codes for other helping professionals, counselors have a "duty to warn" authorities and intended victims when they have a reason to believe a violent crime is going to be committed by a client, or when suicide is a serious issue. Under the federal law governing the behavior of chemical dependency counselors, a warning may be issued only in cases in of possible injury to others in the counselor's agency or to agency property.

This is obviously a substantial variance and one that requires careful thought and consultation should a chemical dependency counselor become aware during a counseling session of a situation in which a "duty to warn" would exist for other counselors. Both supervisors and attorneys should be quickly consulted. While there are obvious risks involved in whatever action the counselor takes, our own inclination would be to warn, making an effort to avoid revealing that the information was obtained during a counseling situation.

The "duty-to-warn" doctrine was spelled out in the landmark *Tarasoff* case decided in California in 1976. It has since spread to most other states. Prior to *Tarasoff*, the ethical requirement regarding situations in which a counselor learned that a client was likely to commit a crime was for counselor notification of appropriate authorities. The decision in the *Tarasoff* case mandated a "duty to warn" not only authorities but also the individuals thought to be threatened. This is the requirement in most states today, but, as indicated above, may not apply to chemical dependency counselors because of the wording of federal law.

In this connection, it cannot be emphasized too strongly that the threat of injury to one's self—suicide—is something that no counselor can ignore or let go unreported. Whenever a counselor has any reason to believe that a client may intend to commit suicide, supervisors or respected peers must be consulted immediately so that a reasonable course of action can be determined. (See Chapter 3 for more on this important subject.)

Managed Care

The privacy problems resulting from the increasing use of electronic transmission of information are linked to the other growing challenges to client privacy rights. Large-scale treatment operations and intervention by managed-care organizations often require a considerable amount of client record transmission from location to location. FAX and phone are now the preferred methods for transmission, all but completely replacing mail and courier delivery. Since it is not always clear who is at the receiving end of these exchanges, the chances for inappropriate disclosure are substantial. Even when the direct recipient of a specific client-identifying record is appropriate, the fact that the number of people with legitimate access to records once they get into an information system increases all the time means that the possibility of disclosure is also increasing dramatically.

The Counselor Is First Line of Defense

Faced with these strong trends it is difficult but especially important for the individual counselor to remember that she or he is the client's first line of defense against inappropriate violations of privacy rights. This means that the counselor must advocate within her or his organization for as much security for client-identifying information as technology allows.

It's important to note that the confidentially principle extends to every aspect of the counselor/client relationship, including maintaining confidentiality after the relationship has ended. That is, it requires that interviews not be recorded or observed without the client's consent, that casework notes and discussion be limited to relevant material about the client and that if the client's specific problems are used for teaching and training, the identity of the client must be disguised. And, once the client/counselor relationship has ended, it requires that records of the relationship be retained or disposed of in a manner that will preserve the former client's privacy.

Informed Consent

Clients may choose to waive their confidentiality rights under certain circumstances and it is frequently necessary that they do so. Perhaps the most obvious situation in which this must occur is when clients are court-ordered to treatment with compliance monitored by a court or criminal justice official such as a parole officer.

In these situations it is necessary for clients to waive their confidentiality rights for this specific purpose by signing a form allowing the counselor or agency to share information. Such waivers must be as specific as possible in respect to the person or organization with which the information is shared and what information is being disclosed.

Most agencies have such forms on hand and counselors must be assured that they are used in all necessary cases and retained in client files.

Both counselors and their clients, whose treatment bills are being paid by health plans, need to understand that the waivers clients sign before beginning treatment give health-plan employees unlimited access to details about the reasons for treatment, including case notes. This access can be intimidating to some clients who choose to pay for treatment themselves rather than risk future disclosure.

Child and Elderly Abuse

Federal law requires health-care practitioners among others to report the knowledge of or observation of child-care abuse, when they "reasonably suspect" it exists, to child protection agencies. According to the law, this should first be done by phone, and the followed up with a written report within 36 hours of obtaining knowledge of the abuse.

Some states also require the reporting of knowledge of or reasonable suspicion of the abuse of the elderly. Unlike child abuse, elder abuse is not one of the exceptions to the federal prohibition against client disclosure, but counselors can report it if they do not reveal the circumstances (treatment, presumably) under which they received the information.

This is yet another instance in which counselors should consult with supervisors and knowledgeable peers before taking action.

Self-Disclosure

Another trend that threatens confidentiality is an increasing willingness on the part of people in treatment to discuss their issues with others. Some authorities believe, in fact, that clients are their own biggest threats to their own privacy rights. This is the case because once a client discusses with an outside person activities, thoughts, or issues she has discussed with her counselor, she has given up her privacy rights on the subject, no matter how inadvertently. Clients should be reminded of this from time to time.

Groups

Additionally, facilitators of groups should remember that they are the only people in the group who have any ethical or legal requirement to maintain the confidentiality of what is said in the group or the identity of the individuals in the group. Groups of recovering people—including AA/NA groups—are both legally and ethically simply groups of individuals who may be morally bound to keep confidential what they hear and see, but have nothing ethically or legally at stake if they do not do so. Since the principle of safety is so important to the success of group therapy, participants should be asked to make a strong moral commitment to protect the privacy of other participants, and asked to renew this commitment frequently during the course of treatment.

Settings

Three final points on this complex subject:

- Treatment-facility managers need to make sure that the privacy of the clients they serve is protected by the environment in which treatment is offered. Counselors' offices must have doors and other means of maintaining conversational privacy. Rooms for group meetings must also be private and closed off from those who are not part of the group.

- Special attention should be called to the need to discuss clinical information about clients only in appropriate settings. For example, hallway or elevator consultations between supervisor and counselor about a specific client—which would be appropriate in a closed office—could result in the accidental disclosure of client information and must be avoided.

Ethical Dilemmas

(After you have thought through your own answers to these questions, see the authors' suggested approach to them in Chapter 6.)

23. Before taking this job, I worked in another treatment program. I recognized a client assigned to another counselor from my work at a previous job. In the staff review of that client, the previous treatment wasn't mentioned. Shouldn't I tell the current counselor about it?

24. At a party, a friend of mine told me he is using the services of a CPA in town who happens to be a present client of mine. I know that my client is still using and the ways in which his use is affecting his work comes up constantly in his treatment. I want to warn my friend. May I?

25. I am facilitator of an after-care group. One of the group members told me that she has learned that another member of the group is telling others what I say during our meetings. What should I do?

26. A client of mine has suddenly started talking about suicide a great deal. He has mentioned it once or twice before, but it has now become a weekly issue. During our session today, he told me he had made a will and had it notarized. What do I do?

27. I have every reason to believe a client of mine is going to try to kill his wife. What is the first thing I should do?

Principle 8: Confidentiality

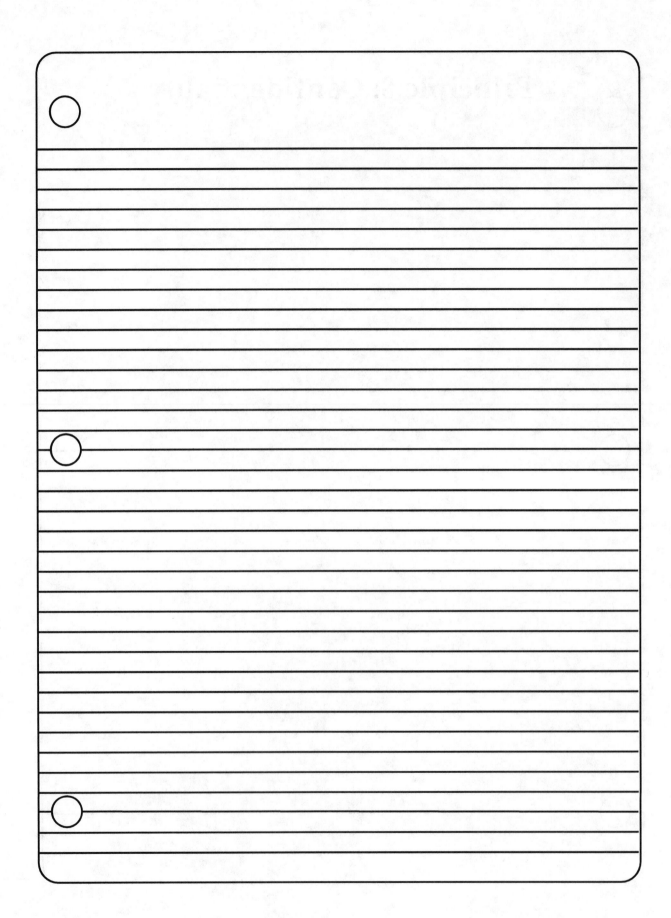

Principle 9: Client Relationships

It is the responsibility of the NAADAC member to safeguard the integrity of the counseling relationship and to ensure that the client has reasonable access to effective treatment.

The NAADAC member shall provide the client and/or guardian with accurate and complete information regarding the extent of the potential professional relationship.

a. The NAADAC member shall inform the client and obtain the client's agreement in areas likely to affect the client's participation including the recording of an interview, the use of interview material for training purposes, and/or observation of an interview by another person.

b. The NAADAC member shall not engage in professional relationships or commitments that conflict with family members, friends, close associates, or others whose welfare might be jeopardized by such a dual relationship.

c. The NAADAC member shall not exploit relationships with current or former clients for personal gain, including social or business relationships.

d. The NAADAC member shall not under any circumstances engage in sexual behavior with current or former clients.

e. The NAADAC member shall not accept as clients anyone with whom they have engaged in sexual behavior.

Discussion

The *underlying philosophy* of Principle 9 is a straightforward one: there should be no hidden agendas when working with a client, nor any other relationships with the client or others that could interfere with the counselor's therapeutic relationship with the client.

The *ethical behavior* required is also straightforward: full disclosure of all aspects of the therapeutic relationship, and the self-discipline to avoid contaminating it with other kinds of feelings or activities.

This ethical standard covers what are referred to as "dual relationships" and is both one of the most important of the Standards and one of the most frequently violated. The basic reason for a strict standard on this subject is that the power of the counselor/client relationship is so out of balance in favor of the counselor that the counselor must take extreme care to avoid even the appearance of exploitation or divided loyalties.

Much of the focus, and quite rightly so, is on the prohibition of sexual relationships with clients—past, present, and future. The reasons for this prohibition seem obvious:

- The strong probability of client exploitation.
- The distortion of the therapeutic relationship by the power of the physical relationship.

The intimacy required for a therapeutic relationship can easily open the door to other feelings and, ultimately, behaviors if the counselor is not constantly on guard. Their addictions have caused most clients to lead emotionally empty and sometimes dangerous lives. The empathy on the part of the counselor necessary to establish a therapeutic relationship can often be misinterpreted by emotionally starved clients as something else. And counselors themselves are in no way immune from these same feelings. When an emotionally starved client is matched with an emotionally starved counselor, the result can be tragic for both.

It should be remembered in this respect that it is the counselor's responsibility to assure that every professional relationship he or she has is kept on a professional level. Clients cannot in situations of this kind be expected to act in their own best interests. Ideally, skillful therapy will turn client fantasies about their counselors into more appropriate feelings. But in some cases this is not possible and when it is not possible counselors need to be able to recognize it for what it is, understand their own vulnerabilities, and seek help for themselves from respected professional associates.

Favors

Though not as obvious, favors other than sexual from clients can also interfere with a therapeutic relationship and must be avoided. For example, counselors should not ask for or accept personal assistance from clients such as washing their cars, helping them move, baby-sitting, or other such seemingly harmless activities. Clients want us to like them and are often quick to volunteer help when they see a possible need for it in order to raise themselves in our esteem. Taking advantage of this is exploitive and, of course, unethical.

Most such offerings of favors—no matter how inappropriate and unacceptable—are innocent enough in their intent. But this is not always the case. Counselors are professionally trained to manipulate their clients into appropriate behavior. Some can forget the extent to which clients can manipulate counselors, and doing favors for them can be a form of manipulation. Drug-abuse clients have spent much of their lives manipulating others so that they can maintain their addictions. They do not easily abandon these skills even when their desire for recovery is sincere. Those who counsel individuals who have served prison terms need to be especially wary of this. Ruthless manipulation is a survival skill learned early and well by prison inmates and not easily forgotten or given up by them.

Counselors should refrain from accepting as clients individuals with whom they have a prior personal or business relationship. These are situations in which counselors both know too much and too little about the individual to be useful. Therapeutic counseling requires a clear and focused view of the client and this makes any relationship other than the therapeutic one unethical, even when the relationship in the past has been of a different nature.

Boundaries

Setting and maintaining personal boundaries are important parts of a counselor's responsibilities.

Our clients are not helped when we treat them as potential new friends. Clients come to counseling in search of professional assistance. This requires respect for their counselors as professionals and human beings, but does not require that they know much if anything about the personal lives of their counselors. Questions about professional credentials and training, of course, should be answered directly. But beyond that, too much transparency on the part of the counselor can be dangerous to a professional relationship.

In an effort to establish the empathy that is required for a successful therapeutic relationship, many counselors will reveal far more about themselves to their clients than is either necessary or wise.

Before a counselor reveals anything about herself to a client other than her name and professional qualifications, she needs to ask herself why she is doing so and in what way doing so will advance the therapeutic relationship. This is the case even when answering a direct question from a client about any aspect of the counselor's life. Before answering a question of this kind, the counselor would be well advised to consider why the client is asking the question or what might be behind it. After answering that question, the counselor will be better able to determine the appropriate response. In many cases, asking the client about the question and what answer they hope for lets us know how to give the best answer, keeping the client's needs foremost in our minds.

As the Standard itself indicates, taping of counseling sessions, use of a client in research, special supervision, etc., are all to be disclosed to clients so that they may choose for themselves their level of participation. This requirement includes disclosure of our own biases with regard to various treatment methods.

Treating Minors

Though it is not specifically addressed in these Standards, a word needs to be said about relationships with clients who are legally minors or adults who have been declared by a court to be unable to represent themselves because of mental illnesses.

The law guides our decision making in all such cases. Treating a minor without parental or guardian consent is often illegal. Counselors should check with knowledgeable persons before doing so, since the law varies on this subject from state to state. Even with parental or guardian consent, treatment of minors and those judged "incompetent" can be tricky because it can often lead to confusion about who the client is and where his or her best interests lie. The basic problem in most such relationships is a possible conflict between a minor's privacy rights and his or her parents' right to know about what is being said in treatment. In general, parents and guardians have an absolute right to know what goes on during counseling. But often fear of disclosure to parents especially inhibits clients from revealing information that is critical to the counselor. The best course of action is to:

- remember the person receiving direct treatment is the client,
- work out an agreement among client, parent or guardian, and counselor about exactly what kind of information will be shared.

Ethical Dilemmas

(After you have thought through your own answers to these questions, see the authors' suggested approach to them in Chapter 6.)

28. A client in my group owns her own remodeling business. She is doing well and her business is not. I know her work is good and I plan to have my kitchen remodeled. I would like to give her the job and feel like it would be good for both of us. What's the problem with that?

29. I live in a rural area with few resources for chemically addicted persons. Everyone knows everyone. What do I do about having friends or people I do business with in my program?

30. I work for an agency that provides treatment for chemically addicted adolescents. During one of our family sessions I met the father of one of the kids I'm treating. We are very attracted to one another and he wants to date me. What should I do?

31. I work with adolescent felons who have been sent to our facility by the courts. The father of one of my clients is constantly asking me what his son is saying about him during treatment. How do I handle his requests?

Principle 9: Client Relationships

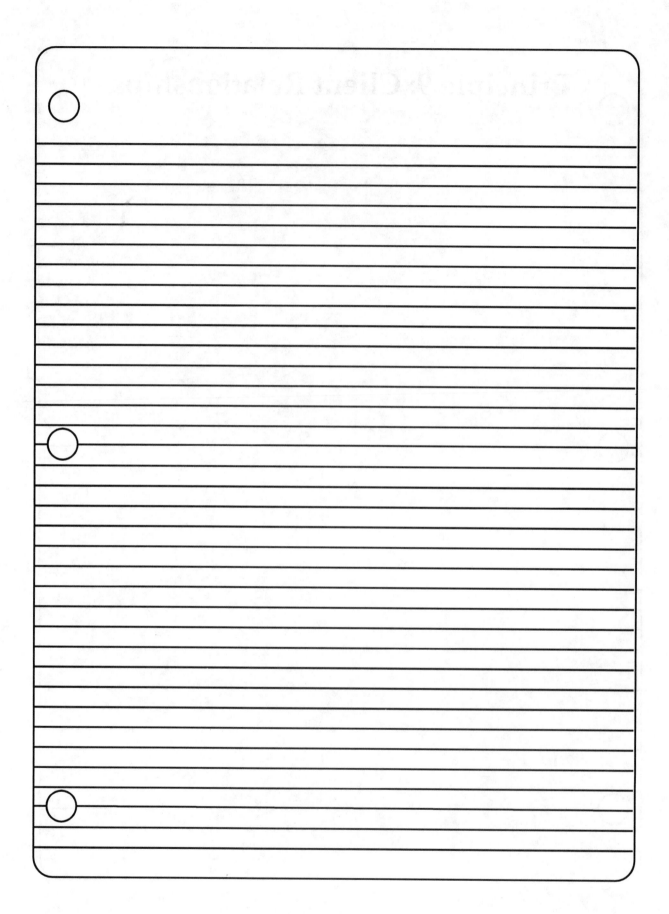

Principle 10: Interprofessional Relationships

The NAADAC member shall treat colleagues with respect, courtesy, fairness, and good faith and shall afford the same to other professionals.

a. The NAADAC member shall refrain from offering professional services to a client in counseling with another professional except with the knowledge of the other professional or after the termination of the client's relationship with the other professional.

b. The NAADAC member shall cooperate with duly constituted professional ethics committees and promptly supply necessary information unless constrained by the demands of confidentiality.

c. The NAADAC member shall not in any way exploit relationships with supervisers, employees, students, research participants, or volunteers.

Discussion

The *underlying philosophy* of this principle is that the people with whom we work are to be treated with the same degree of respect and cooperation that we expect from them and that we give our clients.

The *ethical behavior* required by this philosophy is that counselors must be respectful and fair in their dealings with others with whom they work, including both other professionals and those whose work they supervise or support.

One point singled out in the principle is the prohibition against soliciting clients served by other counselors and, by implication, other agencies. Clients are, of course, free to choose whatever counselors they think may best offer them treatment, but should not be recruited by other counselors when they are already in treatment.

The other point singled out regards cooperation with ethics committees, which is required by the standard regardless of whatever personal relationships may exist between the counselors involved.

Multiple Counselors

One important point not covered by the standard but needing comment here is the fact some clients will have more than one counselor, each of whom is working on a different set of issues. This is not uncommon in cases in which clients have a "dual diagnosis," that is, a diagnosis of mental illness being treated by a mental health counselor and a diagnosis of drug abuse being treated by a chemical dependency counselor (see Principle 3: Competence). And, of course, most clients also have physicians treating them for physical and sometimes emotional problems, as well.

One issue is that different counselors have different treatment methods and client welfare can be jeopardized by real or apparent conflicts among them. Therefore, it is in the individual client's best interest that if more than one counselor is being seen by the client, all counselors are made aware of this fact.

The chemical dependency counselor should find out in the initial interview with a prospective client whether he or she is also receiving treatment from another counselor, and for what. In those cases in which other counselors are being seen, the counselor and client together should determine whether dual (or more) counseling is appropriate. If it is, the other counselors should be notified either by the client or the counselor. Be careful, though: should the counselor assume responsibility for notification, the client must give written permission for such a disclosure to take place.

Many abusers of alcohol and other drugs are also suffering from psychiatric illnesses for which they are receiving treatment. While it is not necessarily likely that the two treatments will actually be in conflict, it is highly possible that mentally ill clients will read conflicts into different treatment methods and either become confused or play off one counselor against another. This makes mutual notification especially important in such cases.

Medications

Besides the possible presence of another counselor, the alcohol and chemical dependency counselor needs to find out in the initial interview about any medications the client is taking and what they are for. Some psychiatrists and physicians treating drug-addicted clients for forms of mental illness will ignore the addiction and prescribe addictive drugs to treat the symptoms of the mental illness. It is not at all unusual, for example, for physicians or psychiatrists treating alcoholics for anxiety to prescribe tranquilizers or other addictive antianxiety drugs.

Alcohol and chemical dependency counselors need to be alert to this and work with the other professionals involved and the client to establish treatment priorities. There is no point in giving drug-abuse treatment to a client who is routinely taking an addictive drug prescribed by another professional for another problem.

In order to protect both the client and the professionals involved, it is far better for the counselor to notify other involved professionals about dual involvement than to leave this to the client. In the process of doing so, all relevant information about treatment—including medication—should be discussed, remembering the need for both parties to receive permission from the client to have such a discussion.

Additionally, counselors should find out what kind of support groups and other forms of self-help therapies are being used by the client. While none of these require notification, counselors should know what kind of advice their clients are getting and from whom.

Ethical Dilemmas

(After you have thought through your own answers to these questions, see the authors' suggested approach to them in Chapter 6.)

32. I've heard some unflattering rumors about the personal life of a local counselor. I wonder if what I'm hearing is true and if it doesn't affect his work. A previous client of mine has happily informed me that he is in a group run by this counselor. What should I do?

33. A client of mine has told me he had sex with the counselor he was in treatment with before coming to me. My client won't confront the counselor or file an ethics complaint. He also has asked me not to tell anyone. I feel like it's my duty to get this counselor out of the field. Is it?

34. When I was a college student working on my B.A. in counseling, my faculty advisor was working on a book about drug-abuse treatment. She knew my interest in this field and asked me first to do some research for her and later to draft several chapters of the book. When the book came out I found that I had written nearly half of it but was given no credit for my work. Isn't this unethical on her part? What should I do?

Principle 10: Interprofessional Relationships

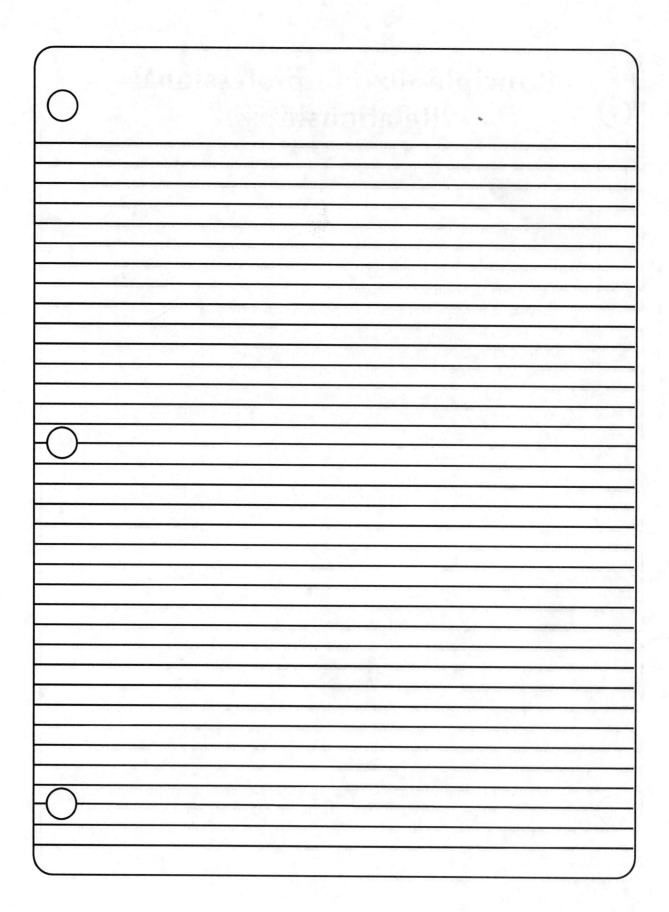

Principle 11: Remuneration

The NAADAC member shall establish financial arrangements in professional practice and in accord with the professional standards that safeguard the best interests of the client first, and then of the counselor, the agency, and the profession.

a. The NAADAC member shall inform the client of all financial policies. In circumstances where an agency dictates explicit provisions with its staff for private consultations, clients shall be made fully aware of these policies.

b. The NAADAC member shall consider the ability of a client to meet the financial cost in establishing rates for professional services.

c. The NAADAC member shall not engage in fee splitting. The member shall not send or receive any commission or rebate or any other form of remuneration for referral of clients for professional services.

d. The NAADAC member, in the practice of counseling, shall not at any time use one's relationship with clients for personal gain or for the profit of an agency or any commercial enterprise of any kind.

e. The NAADAC member shall not accept a private fee for professional work with a person who is entitled to such services through an institution or agency unless the client is informed of such services and still requests private services.

Discussion

The *underlying philosophy* of this principle is that clients have a right to expect that the fees they are being charged for treatment are consistent with those normally charged others for similar treatment, that they have a right to know what the fees are, and that an individual client's ability to pay will be at least considered at the time the fees are agreed to.

The *ethical behavior* required by the principle is that we must set fees no higher than those consistent with professional standards, consider the client's ability to pay, and make sure that all clients understand the financial costs when they choose treatment facilities or counselors.

As is the case with other principles within the Standards, the responsibilities of treatment agencies, hospitals, and the community to provide services regardless of an individual's ability to pay are not addressed by this principle. It applies only to those counselors who have the ability to set their own fees or establish a fee based on their agencies' flexible fee schedule.

But whether or not we have the ability to set our own fees, we have an obligation to keep a client informed about what the fees are and about alternative services within the community that may meet his or her needs more economically, even if doing so may deprive us or our agency of revenue.

Under no circumstances are we to accept gifts, commissions, kickbacks, or rebates for referral of clients to a particular program or counselor. Although the frequency of bonuses offered to client brokers has decreased, we continue to hear of situations where the payment of money or gifts to individuals making referrals still exists, in clear violation of this principle.

Ethical Dilemmas

(After you have thought through your own answers to these questions, see the authors' suggested approach to them in Chapter 6.)

35. In addition to my regular job in a treatment center, I maintain a private practice. My treatment program has no policy about referring clients to counselors like me who moonlight. Can't I refer the people in my group to me for individual aftercare? They wouldn't technically be clients in my group anymore.

36. A large local hospital that offers an inpatient treatment program has a deal with our agency. For every three referrals to their program the agency gets a free bed for an indigent client. And for every six referrals, we get access to their employee facilities, which are pretty lush. Is this ethical?

37. I've been working with a client for the last several months and she's recently started bringing me gifts—nothing big, but things like music tapes and even flowers one time. I'm really confused about how to deal with this. If I accept them, I think I'm in violation of this principle. If I don't, I'm afraid I'll hurt her feelings. What do you suggest?

Principle 11: Remuneration

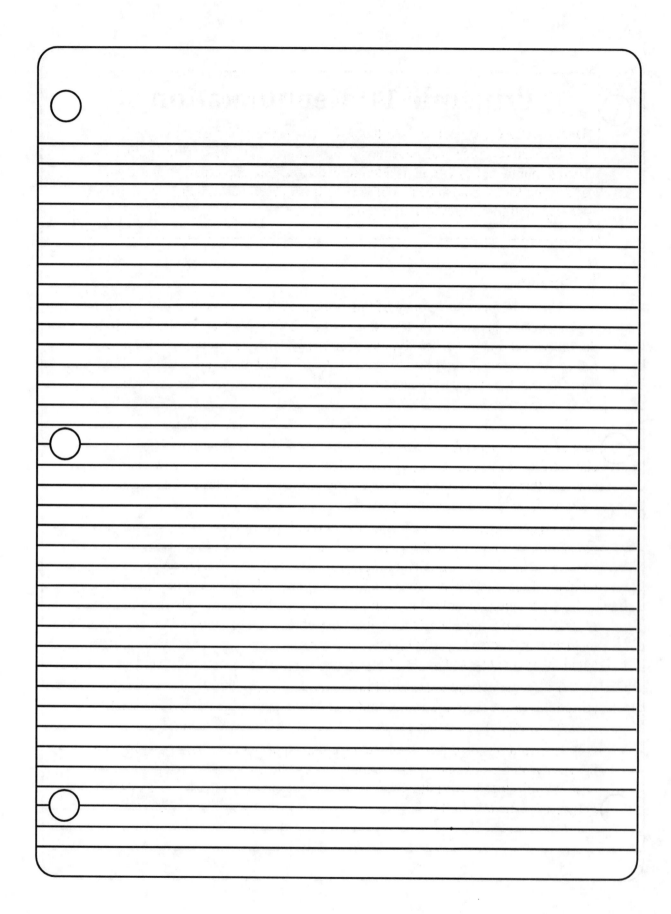

Principle 12: Societal Obligations

The NAADAC member shall to the best of his or her abilities actively engage the legislative processes, educational institutions, and the general public to change public policy and legislation to make possible opportunities and choice of service for all human beings of any ethnic or social background whose lives are impaired by alcohol and drug abuse.

Discussion

The *underlying philosophy* of this principle is that the alcohol and chemical dependency counselor has special knowledge about the effects of drug abuse on the individual, his or her family, and society as a whole as well as about the usefulness of treatment, and that this knowledge should be actively used by all professionals in the field to educate the public and muster support for treatment and prevention programs.

The *ethical behavior* required by this principle is that counselors should accept as part of their jobs a responsibility to be active in community affairs—especially those involving local priority-setting and social-service agency funding—and use this participation to advance programs supporting drug-abuse treatment and prevention, especially among the poor.

Despite widespread public attention to problems relating to the abuse of alcohol and other drugs, the willingness of the public to focus meaningful resources on solving them is not especially strong and may actually be declining. There are a number of reasons for this, including a feeling that addictions are the fault of the addict and should be solved by him or her, a widespread denial about the effects of alcohol, shrinking public funds at a time of increasing need, and other factors that can be addressed by a substantial increase in information to the public at large about the real nature and scope of the problems and effectiveness of treatment.

This principle makes the point that individual counselors should seek out opportunities to use their knowledge and expertise to help make more of their fellow citizens aware of the problems with which the counselor deals routinely.

It should be noted that there are legal limitations on the extent to which public-service and tax-exempt organizations may use their resources to support or oppose specific legislative initiatives. And many agencies have restrictions on who may speak officially for them.

For these reasons, as individual counselors abide by this principle, they need to make it clear that they are doing so as especially well-informed private citizens and not as official representatives of their agencies when this is the case.

Ethical Dilemmas

(After you have thought through your own answers to these questions, see the authors' suggested approach to them in Chapter 6.)

38. The pastor at my church in his sermon last week talked about the "sin" of excessive drinking. I've always kept my professional life and my personal life separate, setting limits on how much time I devote to work and making sure that it doesn't become my whole identity. The pastor's statements really upset me, though. What should I do?

39. My agency is always after me to write letters to public officials and my congressman about various public issues like health insurance for dependency treatment. I don't see the need and wonder if it's even ethical. What's the answer?

Principle 12: Societal Obligations

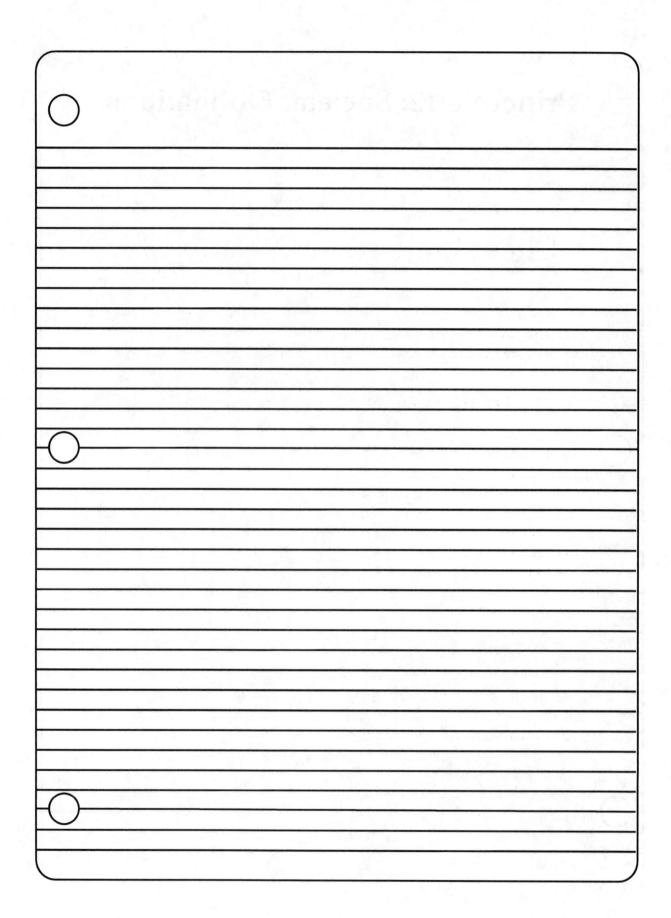

3
Client Welfare and Relationships

There are some further points about the principles regarding client welfare (Principle 7) and client relationships (Principle 9) that should be made here, even though they are not directly addressed in the Principles themselves.

Transference and Countertransference

The therapeutic relationship is an emotionally intimate one. What makes it especially delicate is the fact that it is also inherently one of unequal power. A counseling relationship is one in which at least two people come together, one of whom is in some kind of disharmony and, as a result, seeking help. The other, the counselor, must be congruent and harmonious within himself in order to be of assistance. Although it is presumed that the counselor is farther along this path than those we treat, it is not presumed that we have arrived at emotional and intellectual perfection. Acknowledging this, it is imperative that we have the maturity to objectively evaluate ourselves, emotionally as well as intellectually, especially in relation to those we treat.

The concepts of *transference* and *countertransference* tell us that both we and our clients bring past experiences into the therapeutic relationship that can color our interactions with our clients and our clients' interactions with us.

Originally developed out of the psychoanalytic tradition, these concepts were based on occurrences in intense therapeutic relationships. In *transference,* the therapist encourages the transference—or projections—onto herself of characteristics of individuals in the client's past in an effort to glimpse unresolved conflicts in order to resolve them. The counselor attempts to present a "blank screen," divulging little of her personal reality through verbal or environmental self-disclosure. It is the therapist's responsibility to track and resolve those thoughts and feelings that are stirred by the client so as not to contaminate or influence the treatment unconsciously.

It may be that transference is lessened by the approach to treatment practiced by most chemical dependency counselors, which is shorter term, more educational, and often involves more participation (and therefore more reality) on the part of the counselor than does psychotherapy. Still, we will stir thoughts, feelings, and even fantasies in our clients since all that we communicate, both verbally and non-verbally is funneled through the client's mind and heart.

For this reason, it is especially important that we do our best to keep our therapeutic relationships clean and uncomplicated by our personal realities. That means we must not enter into therapeutic relationships where our own emotional biases or ties would potentially interfere with the progress of the client. This is, of course, the basic reason for the Client Relationship Principle, which prohibits dual relationships of any kind.

Countertransference, in its simplest form, is a counselor's emotional response to the clients he or she treats. These feelings may manifest themselves in both positive and negative ways and either enhance or hinder the therapeutic process.

Some signs of countertransference may include:

- intense feelings of like or dislike of the client
- dreaming about the client
- being frequently off-target in our responses
- a feeling that this is our best or worst client
- boredom or confusion when the client is in for treatment
- emotions about what we are hearing that are stronger than usual
- trouble keeping appointments or letting them run overtime

Countertransference response should not produce shame; it is not a sign of incompetence. Feelings about our clients go with the territory and can in fact aid the therapeutic process while allowing us to grow. In fact, counselors who never experience a countertransference response probably are so far out of touch with their clients' and their clients' needs that they should consider another profession.

In chemical-dependency counseling, we face several special problems that other helping professions rarely confront. Many of us are recovering from the disorders/diseases we treat. That may trigger in us a special kind of countertransference that leads us to respond in a variety of ways. We also believe in recovery. So the "sick" individual we treat today becomes our recovering companion tomorrow. But the prohibition against personal relationships with clients rests partly on the belief that the therapeutic imbalance of power is a permanent one. It also stems from a concern about the emotional health of a counselor who seeks a personal relationship with someone inherently weaker than himself.

As indicated earlier, our clients are not our friends—they are our clients.

12-Step Meetings and Relationships

Many of us who work professionally in the field of chemical dependency support our own recovery through participation in a variety of 12-step groups. As believers in the 12-step model of recovery, we encourage our clients to do the same. It is likely, then, that we will sometimes see our clients at the meetings we ourselves attend. This raises several questions not as frequently encountered in other counseling disciplines: How do I act towards a client in my meeting? What about self-disclosure? Can I sponsor a client who is a member of the same 12-step group as I am?

Here are some thoughts as a guide:

- As professionals, we must honor the delicacy and intricacy of the therapeutic relationship in all aspects of our lives. Clients have the same client concerns whether we run into them at the supermarket or at an AA meeting.

- It is most useful to address this issue before it happens, preparing both ourselves and our clients for a potentially uncomfortable situation. It is important to be clear about our own needs as well as those of our clients. Generally, a friendly but brief acknowledgment is best when meeting a client in a social situation. To either call attention to a client or ignore her may result in an inaccurate interpretation on the part of the client.

- Most 12-step programs follow the basic Alcoholics Anonymous mandate to "tell our stories in a general way." This implies that we save the gory details of our past or present for our sponsor or therapist. If the suggestion "to tell our stories in a general way" is taken, self-disclosure of the kind that might be burdensome should not be a problem.

- Ego is as dangerous for our recovery programs as it is for our clients', so it is critical to remember that when at a meeting we are on equal ground with all present. The tradition of anonymity is a spiritual one which dictates that we leave our status and role, as well as our name, outside the door.

- We must not allow our professional life to interfere with our program of recovery. Too many counselors decrease meeting attendance because of burnout or client attendance at meetings. As a result, too many counselors relapse.

- Although sponsorship may be tempting, it is rarely in the client's best interest. It is important that our clients learn to use their 12-step programs and others in it in order to have a healthy recovery. If we feel we must sponsor someone, it is a signal to ask ourselves why.

Suicide Prevention

Suicide prevention is one of the most important duties of any therapeutic counselor as well as one of the most difficult to fulfill—telling the difference between depression-related ideation and real intent takes exceptional skill and insight.

Suicide is a particular issue for chemical dependency counselors because drug abuse is itself a significant sign of suicide intention. Others are:

- a tendency toward isolation

- low self-esteem/negative attitudes toward self

- a sense of hopelessness and despair

- guilt reactions and psychological pain

- a progressive withdrawal from relationships and favored activities

- sexual-identity crisis

As any experienced counselor knows, most or all of these are characteristics common to drug abusers in general and usually become apparent in treatment. For this reason, identifying a client who is really at risk for suicide requires special care.

There are guidelines to judging the relative seriousness of those who threaten suicide. Counselors whose clients talk of suicide should probe to discover these factors, which—particularly in combination—indicate a high risk:

- presence of a well thought-out plan, including when, where, and how

- has the availability of means ("how") at hand

- threatens immediate action

- "how" is truly lethal (gun, hanging, jumping) as opposed to taking too many pills or wrist-slashing

- isolation with no one nearby to intervene

- previous attempts

- severe reaction to loss or life changes

- relative lack of functionality

- overwhelming feelings of hopelessness, sadness, and feelings of worth-lessness

- lack of supportive friends and family

- chronic or catastrophic illness

This is another situation in which all service-provider agencies should have protocols that are well understood by counselors. It is also another situation in which consulting with one's peers and supervisors is essential, but it is best to do so quickly should the occasion arise.

4
Guidelines for Ethical Decision Making

Ethical dilemmas can frequently be made easier to resolve by approaching them in a systematic way. One way of doing so is to ask and answer the following questions when searching for a solution:

- Is this really a professional ethical problem, or is it a matter in which my personal values and moral code are involved?
- What ethical principle is in question here?
- What is the underlying philosophy of the principle?
- What is in conflict?
    - > Intellect (theory, philosophy of treatment)?
    - > Emotion (feelings about a client or ourselves)?
    - > Needs (physical, financial emotional, intimacy, sexual, status)?
- What are the short-term consequences of this decision?
- What are the long-term consequences?
- Who might be damaged by my decision?
- Who might be helped?
- Whose interests should come first in this case?
- Do I need feedback from someone?
- If questioned about this decision by an objective third party, could I justify it?

5
Ethics for Supervisors

Supervision has a critical role in our personal professional development and in the growth of our collective expertise in chemical dependency.

Because the issues that arise while working as a counselor can be intense and personal, a high level of safety for both client and counselor must be maintained within the supervisory relationship. Safety presumes a level of confidentiality. But like the rules about confidentiality with clients, that mandate that we share certain information if it is revealed (e.g., child abuse or the intent to do harm to another), there are limits to the confidentiality provided by the supervisory relationship.

One of the most difficult ethical dilemmas for supervisors is, "Must I report an ethical violation revealed by someone I supervise?" This question is probably best answered on a case-by-case basis with several thoughts in mind.

- Counselors have a right to a confidential environment in which they can explore with their supervisors personal and ethical concerns that arise while working with clients.

- Supervisors have an obligation to try to ensure client welfare by monitoring the ethical practices of those they supervise.

- Supervisors are required to report unresolved violations of the principals. However, protection of the confidentiality of clients is ultimately a supervisor's responsibility, and no information about a client may be disclosed without written and specific permission of the client, even in connection with an ethical code violation by a counselor.

- It is critical that supervisors openly discuss ethical dilemmas with staff and colleagues before violations occur, offering specific guidelines where appropriate.

- Just as with clients, the limits of confidentiality in a supervisory relationship should be framed overtly early in the relationship. A supervisor must provide a forum for the exploration of professional ethical dilemmas, recognizing that often the supervisory relationship is the only one that exists for such a purpose.

- If an ethical problem arises, the supervisor must immediately seek to resolve it, weighing the best interests of all concerned. If a situation involving a possible breach of ethics is resolved ethically, and if to the best of the supervisor's knowledge no damage has been done, it is probably not necessary to report it. If the situation is not resolved, the supervisor must take action to protect the welfare of current and future clients. This very well could mean reporting an ethical violation to the appropriate credentialing board.

- Just as protecting his or her ability to continue to offer counseling to clients is the first ethical priority for a counselor, supervisors need to look upon assuring the ability of their agency to continue to serve clients as their first ethical priority.

In summary, one of the primary responsibilities of all supervisors is the establishment and maintenance of an ethical workplace. This must be done by both word and deed.

Another is to take seriously the requirement of supervisors in Principle 2 (Responsibility), that says an individual "who supervises others accepts the obligation to facilitate further professional development of those individuals by providing accurate and current information, timely evaluations, and constructive consultation."

Regardless of how long they have been professionals, every counselor needs to be given an opportunity to learn more and hone skills through workshops, college courses, and in other ways. This means allocation of reasonable amounts of time for professional development is as important in its own way as allocating time for direct client service.

The requirement for "timely evaluations" is also important. All employees have a right to know in a formal way how their supervisors rate their performance and what standards are being used for the rating. This is as true for program directors as it is for fledgling counselors. Performance reviews are time consuming and, for some, menacing because a high degree of candor is necessary if they are to be honest and helpful. Because of this, too many supervisors take the position that, "I give performance reviews every day by encouraging or discouraging certain activities or behaviors." This is not enough for a number of reasons, not the least of which is that for the most part the supervisee has no idea of what standards are being used and what aggregate evaluations are. Performance reviews must be:

- objective,

- measured against clearly determined performance standards,
- allow for supervisee feedback and, under some circumstances, change,
- timely.

For all supervisors, it is important that we remember that asking for assistance is not a sign of weakness. It is a recognition of the difficulty of many of these decisions. Supervisors need to develop their own networks of peers to help them sort out answers to difficult ethical questions.

Ethical Dilemmas for Supervisors

(After you have thought through your own answers to these questions, see the authors' suggested approach to them in Chapter 6.)

1. I recently had to fire a counselor for a grave breach of professional ethics. Must I report this to the certification board?

2. One of the counselors I supervise is constantly verbally abusive to his clients. He says this is because they don't follow through on their treatment programs, but I don't think this is effective therapy. Is this an ethical violation and, if so, what must I do about it?

3. One of our counselors who is not a recovering person startled a staff meeting recently by saying that she routinely smokes marijuana on weekends. I took her aside afterwards and reminded her that this is an illegal act. She says there is nothing in the Standards about using drugs on her own time. What should I do?

4. I pride myself on maintaining a highly ethical staff by scheduling staff discussions of real and theoretical problems and by resolving the ones we do face objectively, as quickly as possible and, when appropriate, publicly. Now I have what may be an ethical problem of my own: I am very attracted to a man who was until recently a client of the agency I direct. He is also attracted to me and has asked me out several times. I hesitate to do so, much as I would like to, because I am not sure what my ethical responsibility is here. He has never actually been a client of mine, though because of various staff consultations I am more or less familiar with his case.

6
Authors' Discussion of Ethical Dilemmas

Please note that the authors' discussion of the dilemmas raised with each principle represent our considered best judgment of the issues involved and the way in which they might be resolved. These discussions are not sanctioned in any way by any credentialing authority and the reader may reach a different conclusion on the same set of facts. This is, incidentally, why the whole issue of professional ethics is so complicated. Our major purpose here is to provide a way of thinking about these issues rather than answers that are fundamentally either "right" or "wrong."

Principle 1

Ethical Dilemma 1

I have a long and deep-seated aversion to homosexuals. My agency has assigned a chemically dependent man to me for treatment who has told me he is gay. I do not believe I can develop a therapeutic relationship with this man because of my personal aversion. Must I continue to counsel him under these circumstances?

■ This is a good example of a personal moral position in conflict with a professional ethical standard. The Standards requirement on this matter is quite clear and specific: you should not withhold professional treatment because of your personal beliefs. While there are certainly fewer prejudices than there were a generation ago, most of us acknowledge that we have some in our personal lives. If we were to act on them professionally, countless people who need treatment would be denied it. We need to remember that in choosing to work as counselors and accepting licensing from the state in which we do so we also accept the fact that we must sometimes put aside our own personal beliefs for the welfare of the client and society. Besides, personal and professional growth can result from the resolution of this kind of feeling. Every therapeutic relationship involves learning and growth on the part of both counselor and client. It is quite possible that you would profit greatly from putting aside your feelings on this subject and using this as an opportunity to expand your consciousness and add an important dimension to your life. If reasonable attempts to manage your own feelings fail, you must transfer the client so as not to damage him or you. It is your responsibility to find the most honest and constructive way to facilitate that transfer, doing your best to insure a smooth transition. Not everyone is the best possible counselor for every person.

Ethical Dilemma 2

My agency has established certain minimum payments required of all clients regardless of their economic circumstances. A long-time client with whom I have been making good progress has just been fired from her job and can no longer pay for treatment. What are my ethical responsibilities to her? To my agency? To me?

■ Few of us control the fee-setting policies of the organizations for which we work. However, we have at least an obligation to treat all clients with respect, offering what we can within the limits of our employment and facilitating successful referrals to services which may be available to them in the community at lower cost. In the case of an already established therapeutic relationship, it is also our responsibility to explore all possibilities for continuation within our organization, Many organizations will have payment plans or are willing to absorb treatment costs in some cases. If no possibility for continued service exists, we must handle the transfer or termination with the client effectively, allowing her the greatest possible chance for recovery. This kind of situation underscores the mandate that we continue to advocate for the resources to serve all people, regardless of their economic need.

Ethical Dilemma 3

My administrator has told me to discharge an indigent patient of mine who needs five more days of treatment to make room for an insured patient. I think that is unethical. What should I do?

■ While the pressure on inpatient treatment facilities to fill beds with paying clients is enormous, if the action you describe is potentially injurious to the welfare of the indigent client and truly taken entirely to produce revenue it is clearly in violation of this ethical standard. Remember, though, that the Standard actually applies only

90

to you and others as counselors and not to agencies, as is pointed out in the discussion above. We suggest that you point out the ethical problem to your supervisor, but the resolution of it is actually an ethical issue for him or her and not for you.

Principle 2

Ethical Dilemma 4

I am married and having an affair with a man whom I love very much. He is not a client and is not connected in any way with my agency. My husband travels a great deal and my lover and I are careful to avoid meeting when he is in town or where we might be seen by people who know us. I do not want to leave my husband, but this other relationship gives me more confidence and personal fulfillment than I have ever had before. I do not see how it is hurting anyone or how it affects me professionally. Is it ethically proper for me to continue this affair?

■ Remember that the principle says your own life must be a model of integrity to others. This is often difficult, but its difficulty does not make it less important. How many times have you heard an alcoholic client rationalize behavior you are trying to help her change by saying, "it's not really hurting anyone"? If you rationalize your own behavior with this argument, how are you going to counter it when others use it? There are guilt factors, as well. Will you be able to help a client deal with her own guilt while you carry a load of it yourself?

Ethical Dilemma 5

My agency has not been able to give anyone a raise in two years and I've got a family to support. I have been offered a part-time job running a program for another agency. This would supplement my income with money I really need. I can do both jobs if I use my weekends, sick days, and comp time from my agency to run the program for the other agency. Is it ethically okay for me to take this second job?

■ There are several ethical problems here. One is your responsibility to your agency and to the clients you see at this agency to be on duty when you're supposed to be. Sick days are to be used on days you're sick and if you're not sick you should be at work. If you use them for another job, what will you use when you're sick? There is also the question of whether you can actually "maintain the highest standards" of the services you offer if you're using time you should be using to recharge your batteries for another job. Finally, you have a responsibility to your family to give them the kind of attention they need as well as the material things they need. You can't do this if you're working all the time.

Ethical Dilemma 6

I am a chemical dependency counselor in a drug-treatment facility that is part of a hospital. A long-time alcoholic has come to us for treatment. I believe we can help him into recovery, but only as an inpatient. The problem is that his company's insurance does not cover enough inpatient treatment for alcoholism to do him much good, but he does have coverage for inpatient psychiatric treatment. The people who run the psychiatric unit say they will admit him if we can get this past his insurance company. We can do this by wording our diagnosis to make it appear that he has a number of treatable psychiatric symptoms, though the fact is he does not. If we do this, he will get treatment. If we don't, he probably won't. What is required under this principle?

■ Think back to the ethical hierarchy we suggested in the introduction. This hierarchy says that your responsibilities are first to your ability to continue to work as a counselor, next to society, and finally to your client. In this case, both society and the client's interest would seem to be best served by finding a way for him to get the treatment he needs. The problem is whether your doing so would potentially jeopardize your ability to continue working in the field. That is, what would happen if you got caught falsifying the insurance application? If it would not, we suggest resolving the question in favor of society and the client. If it would, we suggest you resolve it by protecting yourself.

Ethical Dilemma 7

I never use or abuse substances when I'm working or even when I'm about to go to work, but my live-in partner and I do sometimes smoke marijuana and get pretty high on alcohol from time to time. This is always when we're alone or with friends at parties. I'm not a recovering person and my clients never see me using, let alone impaired. Why shouldn't I be able to do these things that millions of others do simply because of my job?

■ The issue underlying this dilemma is one of personal responsibility. Does the responsibility of our role as counselors extend to the lives we live outside the office and job? As counselors, we are the primary instruments of our work, with empathy, integrity and objectivity key components of that instrument. The questions you must ask yourself are: "Can I maintain my integrity and objectivity if I use a drug that is currently illegal in the United States and one that has caused addiction and legal problems for many of the clients I work with?" And, "Will the use of this drug interfere with my ability to effectively assess and assist my clients?" If your organization is a drug-free workplace, you may be subject to drug testing. A positive screen for any illegal substance is likely to cause problems for you and your managers. Many people who are not addicted are able to use alcohol with relative safety and are also able to separate their own personal use from the illness of clients. Illegal drugs use can pose a special problem, however, as you are expected to maintain respect for the institution in which you work.

Principle 3

Ethical Dilemma 8

I have a client who presents his major relapse trigger as arguments he has with his wife about the way their money is used. He has asked me to see them together and act as a mediator so that he can get his feelings expressed in a more neutral place. From what he says, I can see that this dispute would create lots of tension and I think that I could help. Should I see them?

■ Occasionally we will want to meet with the families or concerned others associated with clients with whom we work on an individual basis. This may be stimulated by our need to gather more information, change our intervention strategies, or at the request of a client. It is important to remember that marital and family counseling is a distinct service that requires special knowledge and skills. To present yourself as a marriage counselor without adequate training and/or supervision is unethical. You need to represent the goals of the meeting and your role as clearly as possible if you agree. You should also remember that seeing your client's wife will alter the therapeutic dynamics between the client and yourself. It is important that you be prepared to deal with that reality. You must discuss all possible outcomes of the meeting with your client and consider, in particular, what will happen to your client if your intervention fails. If you have done all of the above, and consulted with your supervisor or a trusted colleague to insure that you are making a good decision, you are ethically safe to proceed.

Ethical Dilemma 9

One of the counselors I work with claims to be recovering and talks a lot about AA, but a couple of times in the last couple of weeks I've seen him coming out of a bar in what looks clearly to me to be an intoxicated state. He's a good friend of mine. Does this principle mean I have to report him?

■ If you believe that chemical dependency is a potentially fatal disease, it seems incongruent not to share your concerns with the counselor himself. If that doesn't work, the traditional principles of chemical-dependency intervention dictate that you, in a constructive and loving fashion, see if others share your concern. If they do, it would be appropriate to go back to the counselor you're concerned about and urge self-examination and treatment. However, remember that the major ethical question here involves the counselor's ability to work as an unimpaired professional. Whether or not his work is impaired by his behavior is a question that must be addressed before formal action is taken.

Ethical Dilemma 10

I was recently asked to make a presentation to a group one of my co-counselors runs. As I was waiting to make my presentation I had a chance to watch him work with the group for the first time. It was apparent to me very quickly that he was in over his head and potentially injuring his clients by opening emotional wounds without allowing any way for them to be closed. I really doubt that he's competent to run this or any other group. What do I do about it?

■ You need to be careful about this. How is it that he is injuring his clients? When you are clear about that, go to the counselor with your information and your concern. Suggest a possible solution and a willingness to support whatever change could resolve the problem. If this does not work, you should take you case to your supervisor. If it is not resolved in this way, a report to the certifying board is needed.

Ethical Dilemma 11

Part of my caseload is an Hispanic-American drug abuser. His English is good and we have little or no trouble understanding the words we use when we speak to each other. But we both get frustrated sometimes because he feels that the suggestions I make to him about changes in his life are things that might make him an outsider in the world in which he lives most of his life. What should I do?

■ This is a common dilemma for counselors in public agencies today, especially those who deal with clients whose cultures are different from their own. One such problem is language itself, verbal and non-verbal, though the verbal part of that does not seem to be an issue here. You and your client have already taken the most important step: confronting the problem. Too frequently, the problem itself is ignored and nothing is accomplished. The reason this step of acknowledgment is important is that it allows your client to explore with you the meaning attached to the use of alcohol and other drugs in his culture and his own specific concerns about living a sober life within it. Successful intervention is most likely to result when you help him frame the behavior required for recovery in terms that are consistent with the realities of the world in which he lives. Also, don't be reluctant to seek help from colleagues who are more familiar with your client's culture than you are. Ask around your agency to find out if others there have similar difficulty. If so, ask your management to provide training that will help all members of the staff improve their skills.

Principle 4

Ethical Dilemma 12

I'm a board-credentialed counselor who has made a specialty of treating battered and abused women. Someone I work with—also a board-credentialed counselor—has been working on a book on this subject, but really doesn't have much experience in this special field. I've given him lots of ideas, but I've never seen the actual book. He now says that his publisher wants the name of an author on it who has lots of experience in the field to give it credibility. He wants me to agree to put my name on it as a coauthor but he says there isn't time for me to read and comment on the book itself. He's willing to share the money with me and I'm reasonably sure he's done a good job. Can I lend my name to this project?

- "Reasonably sure" is not enough in this case. Lending your name as an author implies that you took an active part in the writing and that you are endorsing the ideas in the publication. Insist on reading it first and on the right to make substantive changes as a condition of your agreeing to have your name on it.

Ethical Dilemma 13

The program I work for has decided to advertise for clients for a new codependency group and wants me to lead it. Although I know the basic dynamics of chemically dependent families and have read a couple of self-help books, I've really had no training in codependency. Is this a misrepresentation of my qualifications? How should I handle the situation?

- It is easy to feel pressured by the market or an organization to provide services for which you do not feel qualified. If you are not qualified, you can easily damage others and even yourself by attempting to do so. Although many issues (family, ethnic and gender concerns, relapse prevention, etc.) are covered in the areas of professional knowledge you are expected to have, there is a difference between some knowledge and the knowledge and skills that are required to offer specialized treatment. If you are unable to get adequate training before starting the group, solid clinical supervision by a qualified professional should be made available to you.

Ethical Dilemma 14

My agency provides services to unemployed recovering people, mostly job counseling. Because I am a credentialed chemical dependency counselor, the agency says in its grant applications that we provide drug-abuse treatment. Since I am the only credentialed person here and treatment at this point is not part of my job, this is not actually the case. This strikes me as unethical. What should I do?

■ This is an ethical problem for your agency, but not for you. It might be a good idea for you to express your concerns to the appropriate people in your agency, but their failure to act on your concerns is not an ethical problem for you.

Principle 5

Ethical Dilemma 15

I think it is ridiculous that some people continue to question that alcoholism and drug dependence is a disease. In providing community education, can't I just say that it has definitely been proven that it is a disease?

■ It is important to represent knowledge about drug abuse accurately and objectively. Many believe that the research definitively proves that chemical dependency is a disease. Others do not. Whatever your perspective, you should back it up with research, clinical evidence, and/or the logic that leads you to your conclusion.

Ethical Dilemma 16

I recently took a six-hour course in basic drug-abuse counseling. At the end of the course the trainer said that I and the rest of the class were now prepared to go out and counsel people ourselves. It seems to me after taking this course that treatment is actually much more complicated than I thought it was and I feel less qualified to give treatment now than I was at the start because I have more questions about it. It seems to me that telling beginners like me that we're prepared to give treatment as a result of this brief class is unethical. Is it? What should I do?

■ You should express your concerns to whoever was doing the training. One purpose of this principle is to make sure that people in need of help get it from truly qualified people. Another is to protect our profession from those who could discredit it by overstating their qualifications or understating the complex problems involved in treating people for chemical dependency. This is, of course, the reason for the credentialing process.

Ethical Dilemma 17

I am personally convinced by what I have read and observed that addiction is primarily genetic. When I get family of origin information, I nearly always find drug abuse in prior generations. When I don't, I'm sure it's because the person I'm assessing is either lying or uninformed. Why don't we simply assume that this is true from the evidence we have and find ways to deal with it?

■ It is true that the evidence supporting the genetic aspects of addiction are mounting. Many prevention programs are now based on the public-health model of disease, which includes physiological predisposition as one of the primary factors in the development of alcohol and other drug addiction. The philosophy underlying the principle involved is that it is important to represent all information about addiction accurately, identifying what information is based on feeling, what is based on opinion and experience, and what is reflected in current research. Addressing alcohol and other drug addiction as an illness with genetic and other biological factors is certainly appropriate. It is important to remember, however, that not everyone with a family history of addiction will become addicted, and that not all addicts have a family history of addiction.

Principle 6

Ethical Dilemma 18

I teach a course in counseling to candidates for certification. I've been at it for a long time and have accumulated a number of pieces from various sources that I photocopy and hand out to my students to reinforce points that I make during my training. They're mostly portions of articles and parts of books. In some cases they're things I've picked up at seminars I've attended and I don't even know the actual source. Must I give full credit to those whose material I pass around? What if I don't know the source?

- Whenever we use material from another source, we must give full credit to that source. Over time, many concepts come to be thought of as general knowledge and it can be difficult to separate what falls under the general knowledge category, what are our ideas, and what is the intellectual property of someone else. All efforts must be made to identify the original source. If that is impossible, authors should be acknowledged as contributors in a general way. If you know the material is not yours, but you cannot find the source, you should state that the author is unknown. As you see, this is a two-part process: part one is identifying the identifiable, the other part is not claiming credit for intellectual property not your own.

Ethical Dilemma 19

I've just finished writing a book on treating adolescent drug abusers after working as a counselor in a treatment center for eight years. I've read a lot in the field and kept up with the literature. I believe the basic ideas in my book are mine and I certainly didn't copy anything from anyone. But at this point in my professional life it's not very clear to me what is a new idea to me and what I've learned in one way or another from others. How do I give credit under these circumstances?

- As indicated above, it can be difficult after years of working with chemical dependency to tell what ideas are ours and what are someone else's. Often formal or informal peer review of our material can be helpful. What you gloss over may jump out at an objective reader. And sometimes what you thought was an original idea of yours may be identified with a different source by another well-read professional. If you are fairly sure that the distillation of material is yours, an acknowledgment to the major influences on your thinking is important.

Principle 7

Ethical Dilemma 20

I've been working with a client in my private practice for over a year. For the last several months he has kept his appointments, paid his bills on time, and talks a lot, but I don't really feel like he is getting any better or addressing real issues. I've talked to him about the possibility of discontinuing counseling, and he says I'm the only friend he has. Since it's his choice to come, I've continued to see him, but I question whether I should. What should I do ethically?

- This Principle states clearly that when a client is not benefiting from treatment, that treatment should be discontinued. It seems that your question is really whether or not the relationship with you allows your client to remain stagnant, not needing to find "real" friends because he has you. The fact that he pays should not affect your willingness to confront important clinical decisions. In any decision to terminate a counseling relationship, the effect on the client must be considered and prepared for.

Ethical Dilemma 21

I have been working for several weeks with a client who is new to the agency. She admits that she is a crack addict, but refuses to take any of my suggestions for attending meetings, finding a sponsor, or even taking care of herself physically. I've about had it with her and would like to refer her to someone who might be able to get through to her. May I do so?

■ The referral of an apparently treatment-resistant client to another counselor is a tricky issue. The philosophy of this Principle is that it is our obligation to do everything within our power to assist clients in achieving health and wellness. It states that if a relationship is not beneficial to the client, that relationship should be terminated and the client referred to someone else. But both termination and transfer always carry therapeutic risk, and should be done only after careful consideration and thought. Before doing so, you should ask yourself if perhaps the apparent treatment resistance is the result of expecting the client to respond to an approach rather than trying to meet the client where she is. It is important to assess what your client's blocks to recovery might be.

Sometimes, if we address these blocks or related issues, the client is freed to pursue recovery with them removed. Clinical supervision or consultation may help you identify new interventions that might be more successful with this client by removing the blocks that you are experiencing with her. If, after exploration of all possible avenues, you feel that this client would be better served by a different counselor, referral is appropriate, but you must find a way to make this referral as smooth as possible for your client and without giving her the impression that she has somehow failed.

Ethical Dilemma 21

I am a credentialed chemical dependency counselor and am working on my masters degree. I have chosen as my thesis subject the usefulness of alternative treatment methods and need to do practical research to validate my points. I work in a treatment facility and have plenty of clients I'm sure would volunteer for the experiments. May I use them?

■ The important issue here is the welfare of your clients. Clients must never be used for any demonstration or research that is potentially damaging to them or their recovery. You need to review carefully your research design to make sure that there is no risk involved for participants. Keep in mind that there will always be some kind of effect on your therapeutic alliance when a client agrees to do something out of the ordinary for you: you see your research as a possible advance in learning, he or she sees participation as doing you a favor. This is not necessarily bad, but must be thought through carefully. It might be better to use clients from another agency, or another counselor in your own agency. Although client risk is still an issue that needs to be avoided, it would not complicate your own therapeutic relationships.

Principle 8

Ethical Dilemma 23

Before taking this job, I worked in another treatment program. I recognized a client assigned to another counselor from my work at a previous job. In the staff review of that client, the previous treatment wasn't mentioned. Shouldn't I tell the current counselor about it?

■ The Principle of confidentiality states that you may not share information, except in a genuine life-threatening emergency, without written permission from the client. Therefore, you may not share this information without the client's permission. It would be wise, since this information would affect the current treatment plan, to go to the client and suggest that the client share the information.

Ethical Dilemma 24

At a party, a friend of mine told me he is using the services of a CPA in town who happens to be a present client of mine. I know that my client is still using and the ways in which his use is affecting his work comes up constantly in his treatment. I want to warn my friend. May I?

■ It is unethical to share any information about a client without his or her permission. So, as tempting as it might be, you must not tell your friend. It is critical that we do not share information that would in any way reflect on a client's status with even our close friends and family.

Ethical Dilemma 25

I am facilitator of an aftercare group. One of the group members has told me that she has learned that another member of the group is telling others what I say during our meetings. What should I do?

■ The nature of the what is being told is important to this dilemma. The spirit of confidentiality relates generally to personal information about group participants, including the facilitator. Many times clients share the more educational aspects of what we or others say. For example, a client might share publicly that I am concerned about the use of nonalcoholic beer by newly recovering alcoholics. Confidentiality as an ethical mandate refers to our ability as counselors to keep information shared by clients confidential and to protect their right to privacy in any service setting we offer. The ethical obligation is ours, not our clients'. In general, issues with regard to the breaking of confidentiality by members of a group are best handled within the group. Perhaps you could encourage the person who is concerned to report her knowledge and concerns during a group session. You could offer how you feel about any information that was shared about you and use it as an opportunity to review the confidentiality issue with the group, re-visit trust issues, and help the group decide how to deal with the offender.

Ethical Dilemma 26

A client of mine has suddenly started talking about suicide a great deal. He has mentioned it once or twice before, but it has now become a weekly issue. During our session today, he told me he had made a will and had it notarized. What do I do?

■ You are right to be concerned. A counselor's failure to take appropriate steps when a suicide attempt by a client is suspected is far more common that it should be. Any time a client discusses suicide is a serious time, frightening to both the counselor and client. The fact that your client has mentioned suicide more than once is a red flag in and of itself. Getting his will notarized is an action step that can indicate a movement from thinking about suicide to an attempt. Understanding the signs and dynamics of suicide is an area of competence that all counselors must possess. It is always important to assess quickly and thoroughly the risk that your client may pose to himself. In this case, it seems that you do not yet have this competence. For this reason, you should take your concerns to your supervisor or a respected peer before your client leaves your office. This is a situation that requires assessment and intervention immediately, before the risk for suicide becomes a reality.

Ethical Dilemma 27

I have every reason to believe a client of mine is going to try to kill his wife. What is the first thing I should do?

■ If you believe that a client intends to injure another specific individual, it is your ethical and legal duty to warn the local law-enforcement agency and the intended victim. These are difficult situations, to say the least. If you work in an agency or other organization, your employer should have protocols for evaluating and handling these situations. If there are none, you should insist that some be developed. If you are in private practice, make sure you have a good knowledge of risk assessment, an understanding of state laws and regulations on this issue, and a client relationship with an attorney. The attorney can help you set reasonable guidelines and assist you if making such a report becomes a problem. If you must notify the intended victim and the authorities, make sure all conversations and clinical rationale are well-documented in your case record.

Principle 9

Ethical Dilemma 28

A client in my group owns her own remodeling business. She is doing well and her business is not. I know her work is good and I plan to have my kitchen remodeled. I would like to give her the job and feel like it would be good for both of us. What's the problem with that?

■ We must honor the integrity and delicacy of our counseling relationships in all areas of our lives. Although you would be paying for her services, potential problems could arise. Out of gratitude, she may feel the need to charge you less than her normal rate for this work. If she did, technically you are taking a kick-back. Or, you may feel like you need to pay her more to help her out. Also, what if the job is not done to your satisfaction? Your concern about this could color your therapeutic relationship.

Ethical Dilemma 29

I live in a rural area with few resources for drug-addicted persons. Everyone knows everyone. What do I do about having friends or people I do business with in my program?

■ Professional counseling relationships with close friends and family generally do not work. The subjective feelings of intimacy and loyalty given to family and friends are far different than the objectivity needed to treat clients effectively. Maintaining the role and goals of a counselor with friends and family would be difficult for both you and your friend. If there are really no other options (no other program in town, no other group to be in) you must make the best of it. It is your responsibility to keep the relationship clean and helpful. You will probably need support from a colleague as you deal with your feelings about the relationship.

Ethical Dilemma 30

I work for an agency that provides treatment for chemically addicted adolescents. During one of our family sessions I met the father of one of the kids I'm treating. We are very attracted to one another and he wants to date me. What should I do?

■ The underlying philosophy here is that the purity of a counseling relationship may be jeopardized by personal or business relationships. But there will be some situations where dual relationships with clients are unavoidable: you are not expected to drive 50 miles for a haircut, if the only hairdresser in town needs your services as a counselor. In this case, though, there are some very real problems that need to be thought through realistically. One of the most important of these is that the outcome of both social relationships and therapeutic relationships is essentially unpredictable. On the one hand, if you date this man and it doesn't work out, it would be hard to keep this from influencing your therapeutic relationship with his daughter. On the other hand, if you discover things about him in the course of your counseling of his daughter that you don't want to hear, it could affect your relationship with him. This is a good situation to avoid.

Ethical Dilemma 31

I work with adolescent felons who have been sent to our facility by the courts. The father of one of my clients is constantly asking me what his son is saying about him during treatment. How do I handle his requests?

■ There are a number of situations, and those like this one regarding adolescents are among them, in which we are legally permitted, and in some cases required, to divulge information that could be unnecessarily damaging to the client and his or her relationships with others. In those cases in which it is clear that some kind of response to a request for this kind of information is required, you need to carefully consider the motivation of the person requesting the information, the dynamics of the relationship as disclosed to you by your client, the kind and amount of information that would be useful, and the most effective way to present that information. You should also make sure your client understands your position in respect both to your legal responsibility to respond in some fashion and your ethical responsibility to protect his interests. Your own assessment of the father's motivation and the nature of the father/son relationship should guide the nature of your response.

Principle 10

Ethical Dilemma 32

I've heard some unflattering rumors about the personal life of a local counselor. I wonder if what I'm hearing is true and if it doesn't affect his work. A previous client of mine has happily informed me that he is in a group run by this counselor. What should I do?

■ The underlying philosophy of this principle is that of respect, courtesy, and fairness, using another ethical guideline, the Golden Rule. You could ask yourself if you would want rumors about you believed and then shared. We doubt it. A counselor's personal life is only a professional ethical concern when it affects his or her professional life. If you are truly concerned, you may want to confront the counselor in question.

Ethical Dilemma 33

A client of mine has told me he had sex with the counselor he was in treatment with before coming to me. My client won't confront the counselor or file an ethics complaint. He also has asked me not to tell anyone. I feel like it's my duty to get this counselor out of the field. Is it?

■ No. Your duty is to help your client in his recovery. You would need your client's permission to make any reference to anyone about this. It's clear that your client does not want to confront it and you should respect his wish. If it becomes clear later that this sexual relationship is an issue in his recovery, it would be appropriate to revisit the question about disclosure with your client.

Ethical Dilemma 34

When I was a college student working on my B.A. in counseling, my faculty advisor was working on a book about drug-abuse treatment. She knew my interest in this field and asked me first to do some research for her and later to draft several chapters of the book. When the book came out I found that I had written nearly half of it but was given no credit for my work. Isn't this unethical on her part? What should I do?

■ When presenting information, either clinical or theoretical, it is important to represent accurately both what it is and its source. It is unethical to represent any material as your own when in fact it is not. Many times we may not be sure of the exact source. In those cases, we must communicate that the information is not originally ours. In this instance, it seems clear that you should have been been cited as a contributor. If many students contributed, it would be ethically appropriate to mention in the introduction that the students at your university did much of the research and writing. If the book is already in print, you have every right to request that when it is reprinted or revised your name be added as a contributor. If you really want to make an issue of it and you can prove that you were in fact a major contributor, you could report the professor to the appropriate ethics review board of his or her profession and the university.

Principle 11

Ethical Dilemma 35

In addition to my regular job in a treatment center, I maintain a private practice. My treatment program has no policy about referring clients to counselors like me who moonlight. Can't I refer the people in my group to me for individual aftercare? They wouldn't technically be clients in my group anymore.

■ Referring clients to yourself is always a potential violation of both this principle and the client's trust. Full disclosure of available alternative resources is required at the very least. If there are no other options for the client, or you and he decide it is truly in his best interest to see you, you need to make a clean and clear transition to the new relationship.

Ethical Dilemma 36

A large local hospital that offers an inpatient treatment program has a deal with our agency. For every three referrals to their program the agency gets a free bed for an indigent client. And for every six referrals, we get access to their employee facilities, which are pretty lush. Is this ethical?

- The first part of this seems ethically defensible to us, but not the second part. Getting a free bed for an indigent client seems to be a reasonable barter arrangement. Special privileges for staff does not.

Ethical Dilemma 37

I've been working with a client for the last several months and she's recently started bringing me gifts—nothing big, but things like music tapes and even flowers one time. I'm really confused about how to deal with this. If I accept them, I think I'm in violation of this principle. If I don't, I'm afraid I'll hurt her feelings. What do you suggest?

- Gifts from clients is a problem that plagues most of us. In general, gifts should not be accepted. As with other delicate issues, it is best to have a blanket policy that is made clear to your clients at the start. In the absence of this, a realistic assessment of the motivation behind the gift and the value of the gift needs to be made. It is essential to view all gifts from clients as meaningful in the context of the client relationship; the act of both offering and acceptance or rejection of a gift will carry meaning beyond the gift itself. It is important not to injure the client's self-esteem by the rigid rejection of small gifts. In the case of small gifts or tokens, the culture of your organization or community should be taken in consideration. In residential settings, for instance, clients often present counselors with arts and crafts projects made while in treatment. If this is the norm, and you do not feel it reflects a complex transference issue, acceptance may be ethical and rejection of it may be inappropriate. Many counselors resolve the problem by sharing all gifts with the agency or professionals involved in their practice. For example, a gift of flowers or food can be shared with all. Clients who insist on making gifts of money beyond their fees can make a donation to your organization or another that needs financial support.

Principle 12

Ethical Dilemma 38

The pastor at my church in his sermon last week talked about the "sin" of excessive drinking. I've always kept my professional life and my personal life separate, setting limits on how much time I devote to work and making sure that it doesn't become my whole identity. The pastor's statements really upset me, though. What should I do?

- The spirit of this principle is that as a professional in the field, you need to do your best to confront erroneous information about alcoholism and drug dependence where you find it. In order to prevent burnout, it is important that we all keep a balance in our lives as well as separation of our job from the rest of our life. It should be possible, however, to suggest to your pastor that he avail himself of informational resources in your community. Suggesting or providing materials or courses to your pastor would allow the correction of the misinformation without involving you directly in what could be an argument.

Ethical Dilemma 39

My agency is always after me to write letters to public officials and my congressman about various public issues like health insurance for dependency treatment. I don't see the need and wonder if it's even ethical. What's the answer?

■ Public policy, local attitudes, and legislation at every level of government are important to us as counselors and to our clients. For example, local attitudes and public policy have a major impact on the level of funding for treatment of those who cannot pay for services on their own. And the question of whether treatment really results in sustained recovery is at the heart of efforts to reduce insurance coverage for it. As professionals in the field, it is up to us to inform both the public at large and their appointed or elected officials about the need for and effectiveness of treatment and prevention. It is also in our own best interests to do this so we can preserve and protect our ability to work in the field. The fact that it is in our best interests to take these steps does not make it unethical for us to do so since potential benefits to clients are at least as great as to us.

Ethical Dilemmas for Supervisors

Ethical Dilemma 1

I recently had to fire a counselor for a grave breach of professional ethics. Must I report this to the certification board?

■ It is your duty as a supervisor to report a grave breach of professional ethics on the part of a counselor to your certification board. The board has a process for hearing both sides under such circumstances. Failure to report a counselor would very likely result in a continuation of the practices that led to the dismissal. This would be bad for future clients and bad for the profession.

Ethical Dilemma 2

One of the counselors I supervise is constantly verbally abusive to his clients. He says this is because they don't follow through on their treatment programs, but I don't think this is effective therapy. Is this an ethical violation and, if so, what must I do about it?

■ Principle 7 requires us to "respect the integrity and protect the welfare" of our clients. No matter what the intent of the counselor in this case, abuse is both unethical and poor therapy. You should make this point very clear to this counselor.

Ethical Dilemma 3

One of our counselors who is not a recovering person startled a staff meeting recently by saying that she routinely smokes marijuana on weekends. I took her aside afterwards and reminded her that this is an illegal act. She says there is nothing in the Standards about using drugs on her own time. What should I do?

■ This is a tough one. Strictly speaking, the counselor is right; there is nothing in the Standards themselves that would specifically stop her from using marijuana on her own time. On the other hand, as you point out, doing so is an illegal act. Being caught at it could be highly embarrassing to her, to you as her supervisor, and to her agency, given the nature of her work. While there is nothing in the Standards that would support a challenge to her behavior, your agency might want to think about putting together a code for behavior for all employees dealing with this and other activities that are potentially damaging to the reputation of the agency and the profession.

Ethical Dilemma 4

I pride myself on maintaining a highly ethical staff by scheduling staff discussions of real and theoretical problems and by resolving the ones we do face objectively, as quickly as possible and, when appropriate, publicly. Now I have what may be an ethical problem of my own: I am very attracted to a man who was until recently a client of the agency I direct. He is also attracted to me and has asked me out several times. I hesitate to do so, much as I would like to, because I am not sure what my ethical responsibility is here. He has never actually been a client of mine, though because of various staff consultations I am more or less familiar with his case.

■ As you know as a supervisor, the rationale for not having intimate and/or sexual relationships with clients is rooted in the inherent inequality between the two. Healthy intimacy can take place only in the context of a relationship where there is little difference in power. Although this client was not specifically a client of yours, your role with regard to his case places you in a position in which his power is not equal to yours. You have been privy to information about him and have been in a position to influence the course of this treatment. As a result, pursuing a personal relationship with him is not recommended. Also important to consider is your relationship and role with the staff you supervise. Having a personal relationship with a current or recent client of someone on your staff would likely complicate your role as supervisor and your staff's view of you. It would be interesting to know what your staff would say if you were to ask them about this. It is important in these complex situations to think through all possible outcomes, including your ability to justify your decision to an objective third party should it be questioned. We also recommend that you discuss the situation with a mature and trusted colleague.

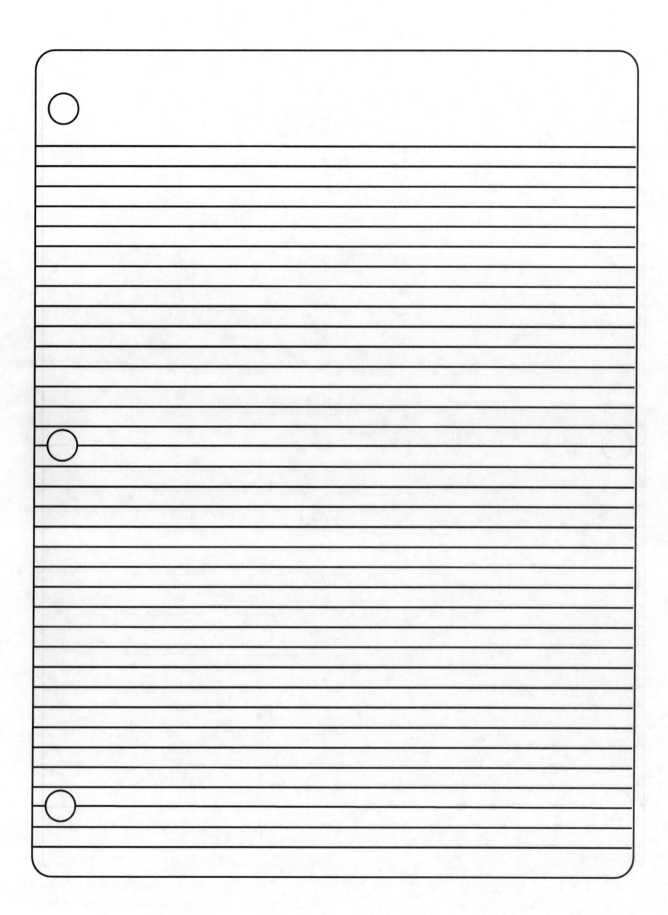

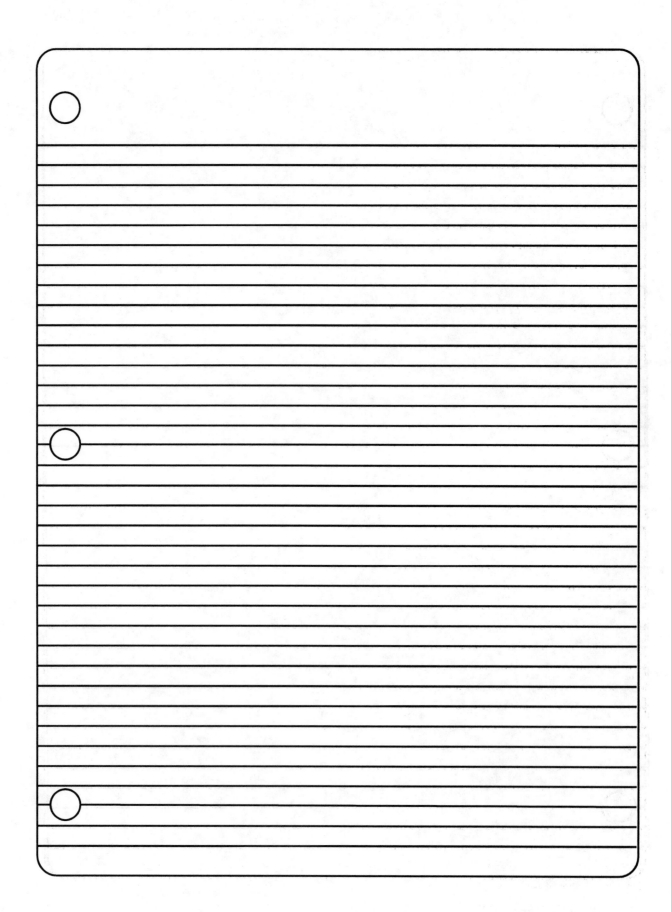

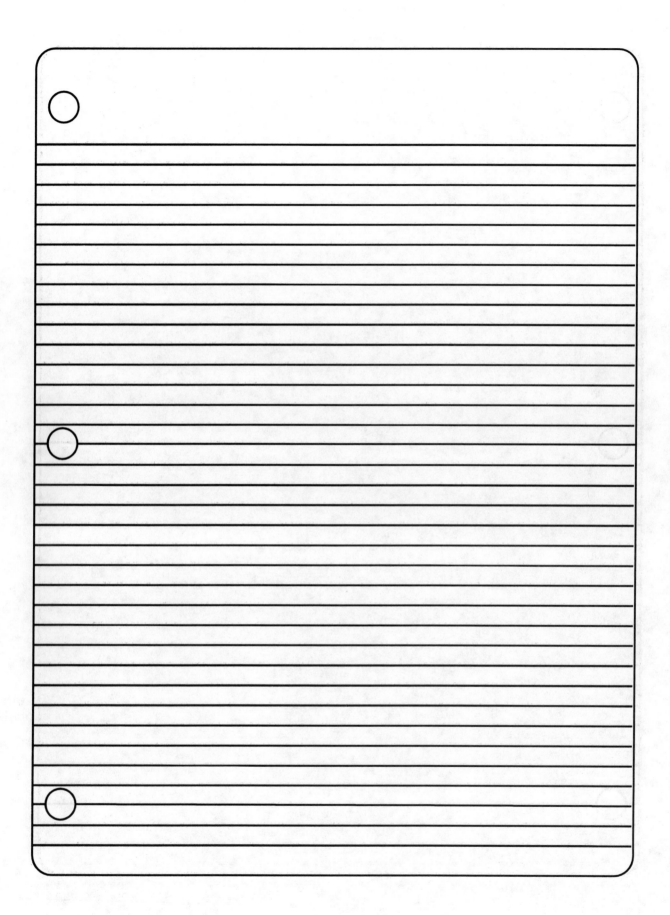

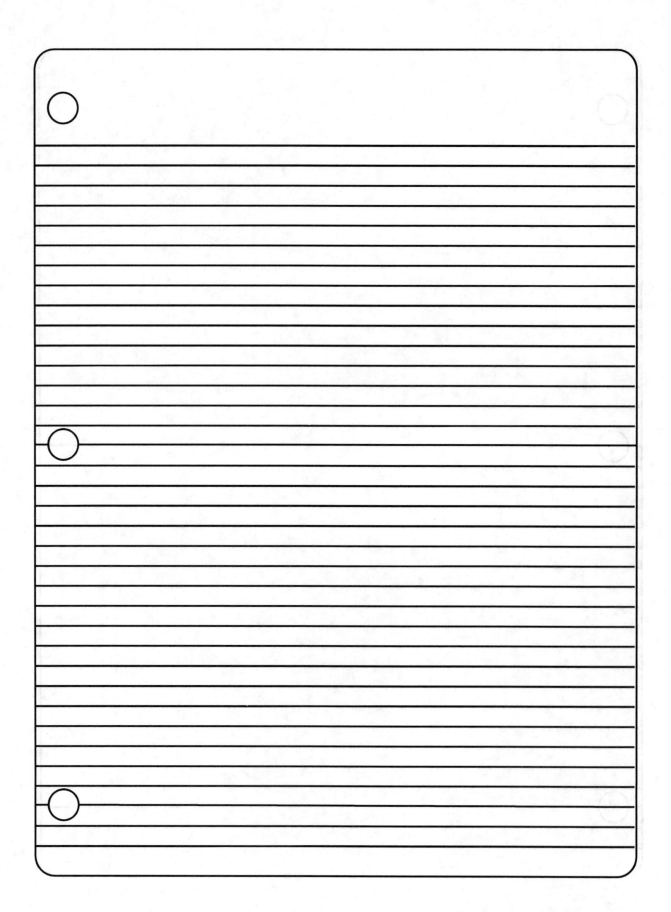

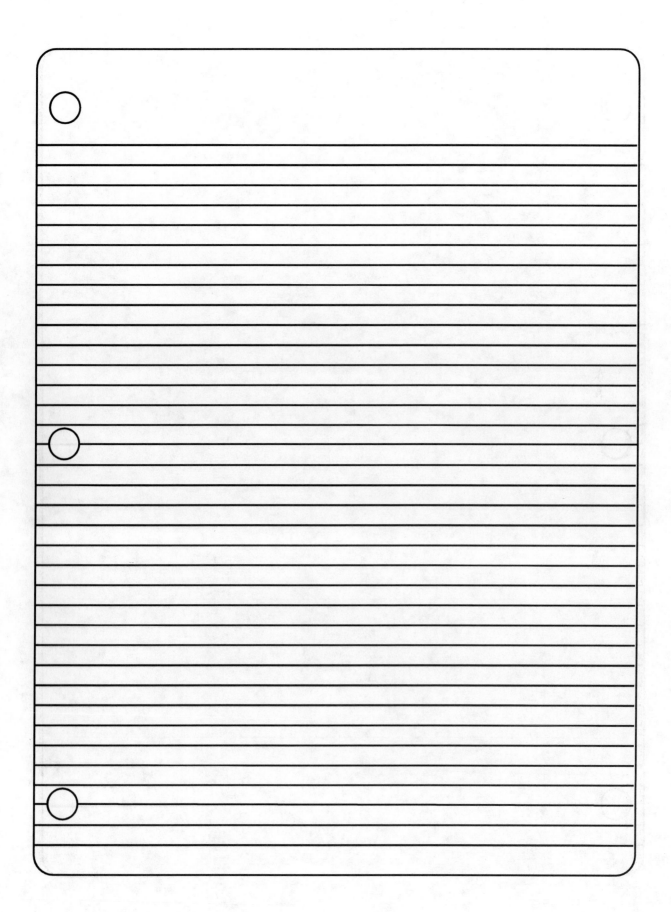

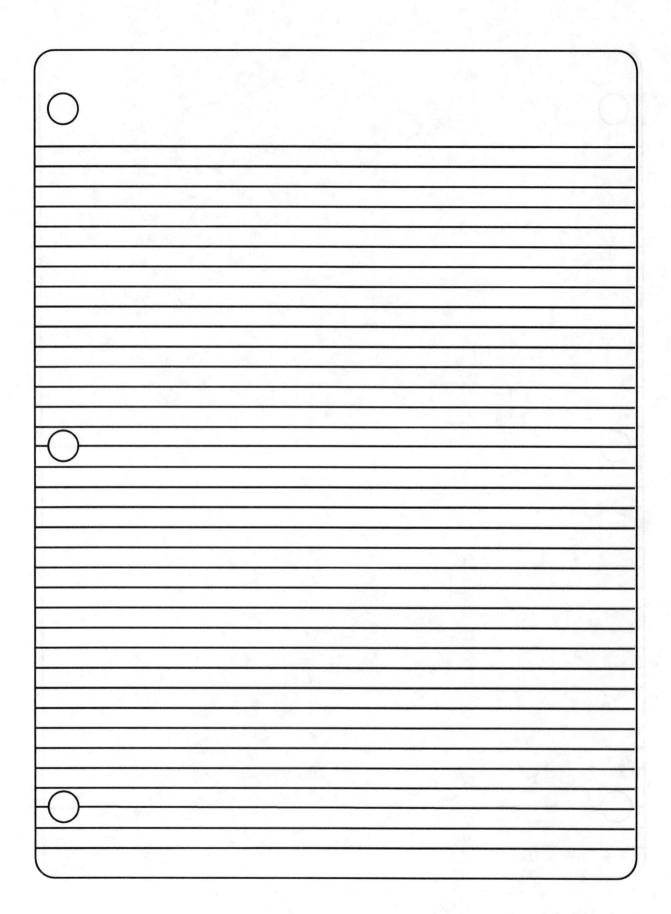

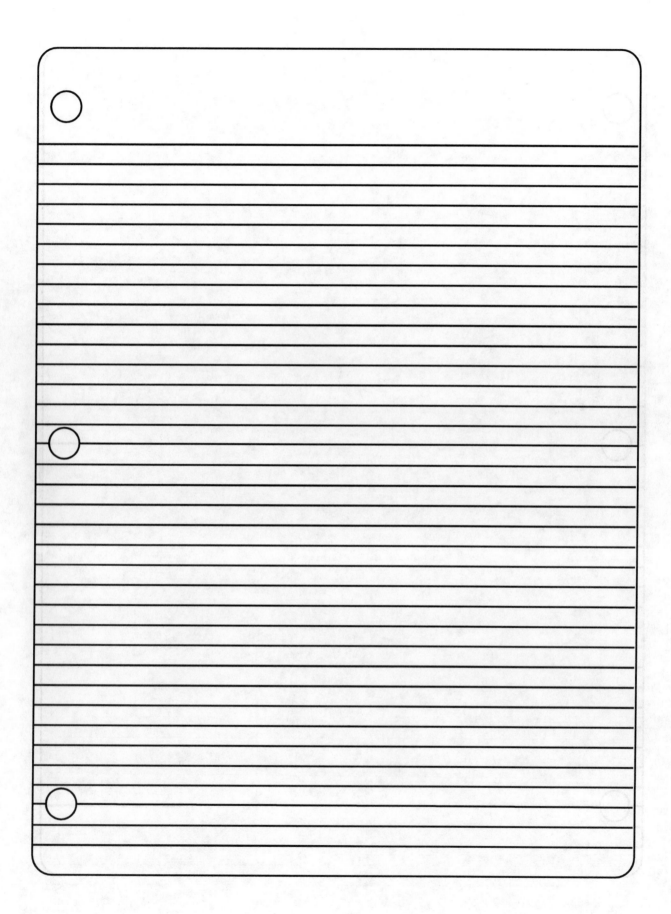

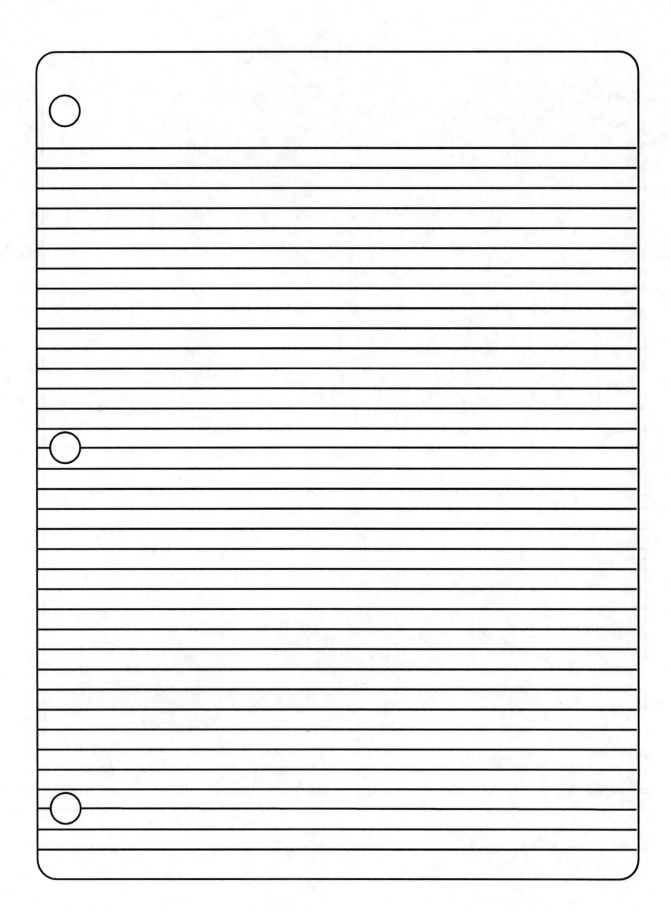